Polyphemus, the one-eyed Cyclops

Children's BOOK OF
Mythical Beasts &
Magical Monsters

DK

Penguin
Random
House

Senior designer Sonia Whillock-Moore
Senior editor Deborah Lock
Additional editing by Lee Wilson
and Lorrie Mack
Additional design by Lauren Rosier,
Poppy Joslin, Jemma Westing, Hedi Hunter,
Clare Patane, Rachael Foster, Rosie Levine
Art director Martin Wilson
Publishing manager Bridget Giles
Production editor Siu Chan
Production controller Claire Pearson
Jacket editor Matilda Gollon
Managing jackets editor Saloni Singh
Jacket designer Laura Brim,
Suhita Dharamjit and Dhirendra Singh
Jacket design development manager
Sophia MTT
Picture researcher Jo Walton

Myth consultant Neil Philip

First published in Great Britain in 2011 by
Dorling Kindersley Limited
80 Strand, London WC2R 0RL

A CIP catalogue record for this book
is available from the British Library.

ISBN 978-0-2411-8941-2

Printed and bound by Leo, China

Discover more at
www.dk.com

How to use this book

In this book, find out about myths, legends,
and folklore from countries around the
world; read the stories, find out about
the characters, and compare their themes.
There are four different types of pages
in this book:

*AROUND THE WORLD: Wonder at the
similarities and common elements in myths
from around the world.*

*WHO'S WHO: Find out about the relationships
between gods of certain cultures and the
characters that feature in famous legends.*

*TELLING THE TALE: Discover the excitement
and drama of myths that have been passed
down from generation to generation.*

*CHARACTER UP CLOSE: Take a close-up look
at mythological characters, how they are
depicted, their role, and their adventures.*

Contents

What are myths?

Myths are Stories

Though the tales seem very different, all myths and legends have very similar elements. Characters, some good, some bad, have adventures or journeys in amazing settings. There are obstacles and challenges to overcome and an epic ending that neatly tidies up loose ends.

Myths are timeless

Myths have been around for thousands of years – that's way before books were invented! Myths were passed on from generation to generation by elders, priests, parents, and storytellers. Myths have endured for so long because of their meanings, lessons, and in some cases, their sacred nature.

Myths are entertainment

Myths have lasted so long because they are entertaining. If they were dull and boring they would be easily forgotten. Instead myths have influenced storytelling for thousands of years. The stories you read, such as *Harry Potter*, and the movies you watch today, such as *Star Wars*, all borrow elements from myths and legends.

Myths are aRt

The great characters of myth and legend have inspired artists for centuries. The creative worlds of the myths have been immortalized by sculptures and paintings showing epic clashes of good verses evil.

Myths, legends, and folklore use stories to explore human lives, the natural world, and also the unseen spiritual world. Stories of gods, heroes, demons, and monsters offer insights into the great unanswerable questions of life.

Myths are Lessons

Before there was such a thing as school, children learnt from their parents and elders in the community. They used stories to pass on knowledge in a way children would understand. These stories had meanings and lessons that the children could learn from. Societies told their own myths to reflect their environment and culture, and explain the things they could not understand.

Myths are understanding

Myths aren't just gentle tales to educate children. They are also ways for people to understand the world around them. Before science, explanations of the world were based on superstition and fear. Myths, legends, religion, and folklore try to explain the unknown, such as earthquakes, the Sun, and death.

Myths are not...

... proven. Their origins are lost in time, and no one really knows why they were first told. They have been told by many storytellers over thousands of years. Like a game of Chinese whispers, they never remain quite the same. A snake may become a serpent, then a dragon, and finally a triple-headed beast! True or not, myths and legends are still relevant and can teach us much about the world today.

Nature and nation

Just like us, early people wanted to understand themselves and the world around them. Each culture had its own explanations about how the universe began and what happened next…?

A painting from the Book of Marvels, *written in the 13th century about the stories told by the merchant Marco Polo when he travelled across Asia.*

In the beginning

Every culture has a **creation story** to explain how the world was made. Many myths speak of a world of **chaos** out of which the **world** was formed. Others tell of the world hatching from an egg, or being created on the back of an animal.

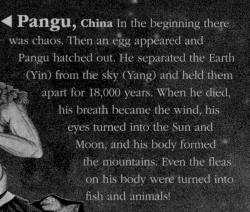

◀ **Pangu,** China In the beginning there was chaos. Then an egg appeared and Pangu hatched out. He separated the Earth (Yin) from the sky (Yang) and held them apart for 18,000 years. When he died, his breath became the wind, his eyes turned into the Sun and Moon, and his body formed the mountains. Even the fleas on his body were turned into fish and animals!

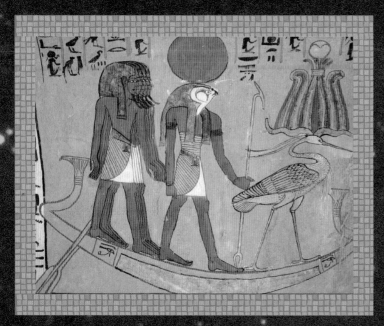

◀ **Benu bird,** Ancient Egypt Shown as a long-legged heron, the Egyptian benu bird flew across the waters of non-being at the first dawn. Landing on a rocky pyramid, poking from the water, it let out a harsh cry, shattering the eternal silence and waking up the world.

◀ **Seneca nation,** North America Once the world was one of sky and a great expanse of water. First woman fell from the sky world into the waters below, but was rescued from drowning by the sea animals. The toad dived for mud on the seafloor, and put it on the turtle's back to make land for her. A Cherokee myth has a similar tale of a water beetle diving to collect mud to make the Earth, while the Algonquian myths have a muskrat.

▶ **The Dreaming,** Australia When the Dreaming came, all the creating ancestors of the world woke up and shaped the land. Australian Aborigines can still enter the Dreaming through storytelling, rituals, and art. It is not past, but eternally present.

◀ Muspelheim, Norse

Once there were two lands separated by a dark empty space called Ginnungagap. The light and heat of Muspelheim and the dark, icy cold of Niflheim met, melting the ice and producing a giant frost ogre, Ymir (see page 49). Later, Ymir was killed by the first people and his body became the Earth.

SEEING THINGS
For more about mythical Norse lands see page 90.

▲ Eurynome and Orphion, Ancient Greece

In one version of the creation story, the goddess Eurynome emerged from a dark void and turned into a dove. She laid an egg and a giant serpent Orphion coiled around it. The warmth of his body caused the egg to hatch and out came the sky, mountains, seas, and rivers.

◀ Aido-Hwedo and Mawu, West Africa

The female creator god, Mawu, created people. Then, with the help of the male serpent Aido-Hwedo, she made the world. Travelling in huge circles, they made the Earth in the shape of a calabash (a round fruit). The snake's winding motion carved out rivers and valleys, and minerals and mountains were formed from waste expelled from his body.

13

The ever-hungry Raven was a very important mythical hero of the west-coast tribes, as he was said to have seeded the world with the plants and fish needed for survival. Many of their myths are about him, and there are lots of different versions of each one.

Raven tales
International character
All around the world, and particularly in North America, Europe, Scandinavia, and Siberia, ravens appear in traditional stories and myths.

Ancient advisors
In Norse legend, the chief god, Odin (see page 91), is often described or pictured with two ravens, Huginn (meaning "Thought") and Muninn (meaning "Memory"), who served as his eyes and ears. They are sometimes shown sitting, one on each of his shoulders.

Russian trickster
In the far eastern part of Russia and the Russian Arctic, Kutkh the raven spirit is not only a creation figure, he is also an ancestor of mankind, a powerful shaman (or witch-doctor), and a cunning trickster. Some of the raven stories from this area are very similar to the raven tales of native North America.

Ravens in the Tower
For hundreds of years, people have believed that if the ravens ever leave the Tower of London, England will suffer a terrible disaster. To this day, ravens are kept and protected there to avoid this happening.

The Raven who stole the light

Throughout their history, the first-nation tribes on the west coast of Canada (including the **Haida** and the **Tlingit**) have woven myths about Raven – a magical trickster who has lived on Earth for all time.

When the world was very new, there was absolutely no light – everybody lived in the dark. To get from place to place, hunt and fish, and even find berries for food, people had to reach out and feel for familiar trees, rocks, water, and bumps in the ground.

There was no light because the selfish Sky Chief kept it all hidden away in a box, which he kept close to him in his big house. This made Raven very angry, so he worked out a plan to sneak inside the Chief's house and steal the box. To do this, he first turned himself into a tiny pine needle. When the Chief's beautiful daughter went to a nearby spring to fetch water, Raven rode on the breeze and dropped into her jug. When she drank the water inside, the pine needle slipped smoothly down her throat.

Once Raven was inside her, he changed himself into a human baby waiting to be born. When the tiny boy arrived, he had raven-dark hair, shiny black eyes, a beaky nose, and a harsh, crow-like cry, but the Sky Chief was completely charmed by him, and did everything he could to make him happy. For many weeks, Raven lived as a gurgling baby, playing with his mother and his grandfather in their house.

One day, catching sight of the hidden box that held the world's light, he reached out to grab it. The Sky Chief snatched it away quickly, but the baby cried and cried and cried until his grandfather gave in – as adoring grandfathers often do.

As soon as the treasure was in his hands, Raven opened it and released the magic ball of light. Instantly, he turned back into a bird, snatched the ball in his beak, and flew away through the house's smoke hole and up into the sky. As he passed over many mountains, rivers, and oceans, he grew weary and dropped half the light. It shattered into a thousand pieces, which became the stars and the Moon. In the end, exhausted by his travels, Raven let go of all the remaining light and it filled the sky. His precious load had turned into the Sun.

CHARACTER UP CLOSE

Biography
Mama Quilla, Mother Moon

Titles
Also known as Mama Kilya, she was the goddess of the Moon, marriage, feasts, and the protector of women.

Family connections
She was the daughter of Viracocha, the Creator god, and Mama Cocha, the Mother Sea. She was sister to and the wife of Inti, the Sun god.

Her children were Manco Capac (see picture below) and Mama Ocllo, who were sent to the shores of Lake Titicaca to teach the people and establish laws. They are known as the mythical founders of the Inca empire.

More children
Also in later myths she became the mother of Pacha Camac, the Earth-maker. His wife was the popular goddess, Pacha Mama, Earth-mother, who protected crops and caused earthquakes.

Pacha Mama was very important to the people who lived in the Andes mountains.

Mama Quilla

Mama Quilla, the goddess of the **Moon**, was the third most powerful god of the Incas. They were a warrior tribe of Peru, **South America**. Between the 1200s and the 1500s, their empire expanded all along the Andes mountain range, and as other tribes were **conquered**, their gods and goddesses were included and combined with the Incas' stories.

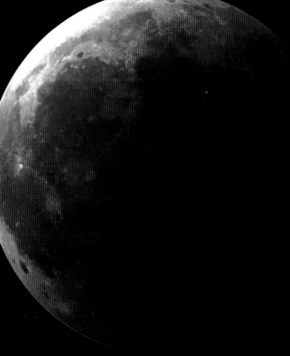

Lunar eclipses

The Incas were afraid of lunar eclipses as they believed that they were caused by a wild animal (possibly a mountain lion, serpent, or puma) attacking Mama Quilla. During the eclipses, they would try to scare away the animal by throwing weapons, waving their arms, and shouting. They believed that if the animal succeeded, the world would be left in darkness.

A lunar eclipse happens when the Earth blocks out the Sun's light shining on the Moon.

The Sun God

The most important Inca god was Mama Quilla's husband and brother, Inti, the Sun. He was the father of the Inca ruler, and the special protector of the Inca people. In his temple, Inti was worshipped in the form of a golden disc with a human face.

The Incas thought of gold as the sweat of the Sun.

16

Mama Quilla had a round face, like a full moon, which symbolized beauty.

The Incas believed that the silver they found was the tears of the goddess, which fell to the Earth.

If you look at the Moon you can see dark spots. According to a legend of the Incas, these were formed when a fox who fell in love with Mama Quilla went to visit her, and she squeezed the creature against her.

TELLING THE TALE

Epic Japanese tales
The first gods
In the beginning, the lighter parts of the swirling chaos floated upwards and formed Takama-ga-hara, the High Plain of Heaven. The first forces were created in the form of three invisible gods who dwelt in the heaven. A reed grew upwards through the chaos and from its top two more gods appeared. Then other generations followed. Izanagi and Izanami were the last of these heavenly gods.

The feud
Their eldest daughter, Amaterasu, was born so bright that she was sent to the heavens to shine light on the Earth. Once she had warmed the Earth, she showed the people of Japan how to grow rice and wheat and use silk worms to make cloth. But, her brother Susano-O annoyed her when he destroyed her home and crops so she shut herself away in a cave.

The rising Sun
The world was in darkness, until the other gods in desperation tricked her to come out. Some say they showed her a mirror and thinking it was a new goddess, and not her reflection, she came out. Others say the gods made lots of noise as if they were having a party and being curious to find out what was going on, she came out. When she appeared, light was brought back into the world.

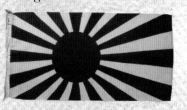

For many years the Japanese flag showed a rising sun, symbolizing Amaterasu coming out of the cave.

The first emperor
Amaterasu sent her grandson Ninigi to rule over the land and gave him three treasures – a jewelled necklace for kindness, a mirror for purity, and a sword for courage. These are the symbols connected to the royal household of Japan. According to legend, his great grandson Jimmu-Tenno became the first emperor.

A *nation* born

In Japanese myths, the creation of the universe began with two gods, Izanagi and Izanami, who were brother and sister. They descended from the heavens on a floating rainbow bridge. Below them was **chaos** – a swirling oily darkness. Standing on the bridge, Izanagi stirred the chaos with a jewelled spear until an island formed

Creation had begun. The first island was called Onokoro. To continue creating, Izanagi and Izanami decided to marry. They built a tall column on the island for their marriage ceremony. Izanagi went one way and Izanami went the other way around the column and when they met they said their vows. However, the bride, Izanami, spoke first. This upset the gods in heaven for the bridegroom Izanagi should have said his wedding vows first.

They repeated the ceremony properly, but Izanami was now destined to give birth to demons and monsters as well as to gods and spirits.

Together they created the eight islands of Japan and all the plants and animals. Izanami gave birth to the gods and spirits who would be responsible for them, including Amaterasu, the Sun goddess, Tsuki-yomi, the Moon god, Susano-O, the storm god, and many other gods of nature, oceans, lowlands, and mountains. Izanami was destined to die and so, when Kagutsuchi, the fire god, was born, she died in his flames and descended to Yomi, the underworld. In grief, Izanagi went to the underworld after her.

18

Yomi, the land of the dead

Over 80,000 demons were said to live in the dark dismal land of the dead, Yomi. Their job was to carry the dead to Emma-O, the ruler and judge, who lived in an underground castle. Good people were reborn, while evil people were sent to Yomi. There they would be tortured until their dead bodies rotted away by maggots and turned into demons, too.

He pulled a comb from his hair and lit it. In horror, he saw that he was too late to save her as she had turned into a rotting corpse and her body was covered in maggots.

Izanami was furious that her husband had seen her and ordered the demons to chase him. Izanagi fled, throwing his headdress and comb behind him. The headdress turned into grapes and the comb into bamboo shoots, which the demons stopped to eat. However, Izanami was close on his heels. Only just in time, Izanagi reached the entrance and rolled a vast stone across it, separating the living and the dead forever.

CREATE SOUND EFFECTS

Gather a collection of sound-making objects from around your home to create sound effects as you retell the story. You could swish a bottle filled with water for the swirling chaos, make tinkling chimes using knives and forks for the wedding cermony, and bang saucepans with wooden spoons for the demon chase.

Biography
Rainbow snake

Creator serpents

The Kunwinjku-speaking (Gunwinggu) people of western Arnhem land, northern Australia, speak of two serpents. Yingarna, is the creator being. Her son, Ngalyod created the mountains, valleys, and waterholes. He lives at the foot of waterfalls and looks after Yingarna's children.

Yingarna

Yingara is believed to have come from the east. She carried baskets full of the people she had created and left a group of them at each of her resting places. Sometimes she appears as a rainbow snake and other times as a woman.

Rock paintings depicting this ancestral figure date back thousands of years.

Shapechanger

Rainbow snakes do not always appear as either rainbows or snakes. In stories they may seem almost human. In art, they may borrow parts from other animals, such as this rainbow snake with the head and tail of a crocodile.

Rainbow snake

Rainbow snakes play an important part in the beliefs of the **Aboriginal peoples** of Australia. They are male and female creative powers of *The Dreaming* (see page 12) and their bodies shaped the mountains and river valleys. Closely associated with **rain, waterholes, and rainbows,** they are the source of magical powers.

The rainbow's end

Aboriginals in Queensland say that the rainbow is the rainbow snake leaping between waterholes. At the place where the rainbow touches the ground, quartz crystals are formed. These crystals may also appear within an individual, who is then destined to become a "clever person" – a wise person with special knowledge.

Legend has it that the rainbow snake must not be disturbed when he is arching across the sky.

"Serpent Dreaming" Aboriginal painting

Mother and father

There are many rainbow snakes in Aboriginal myth, but the eternal rainbow snake, the source of life, is called both the "Great Father" and the "All-mother". When it spits, it rains, and its voice is thunder. Each Aboriginal people has their own name for the snake. It is called Yurlungul in Arnhem Land, and Wollunqua in central Australia.

Guardian of the waterholes

The rainbow snake has life-giving powers. He is linked with creation, the growth of plants and animals, plentifulness, and rebirth.

The rainbow snake sleeps in waterholes and causes floods when he awakes and stretches out.

The rainbow snake sends storms and floods as punishment to those who break the law of the Earth.

He swallows people during floods and turns their bones into stone.

The rainbow snake has power over life and death. He can enter people and give them magical powers, or leave little rainbows inside them to make them ill and die.

21

Maori gods

Ancient Maoris saw themselves and their lives closely linked together with **nature**. Therefore, they had gods for each of the many aspects and elements of nature. They would not fell a tree or go hunting without first **honouring** the appropriate god.

The family feud

The children of the first pair of gods, Rangi and Papa, lived in darkness and could not see anything. This was because their parents – the Sky and the Earth – clung together letting no light escape. Annoyed, the children (all except Tawhiri, the god of weather) plotted to work out how to separate their parents to create night and day. After many attempts by them, Tane, the god of the forests, pushed against his parents with his mighty feet and gradually lifted them away from each other. Their parents cried in anguish, and Tawhiri in his anger, uprooted trees and whipped up the seas, causing creatures to hide away and different landscapes to form.

Tane, the god of the forests

Rangi, the Sky Father, and Papa, the Earth Mother, at first clung together in the dark.

Shamed

Once everything settled down peacefully again after the separation of Rangi and Papa, Tane created a woman from clay and breathed life into her. She was called Hine-hau-one, meaning the "Earth-formed Maiden". They had a daughter named Hine-titama, meaning "Dawn Maiden". Unaware of who her father was, she married Tane and they had many daughters. When Hine-titama found out the truth, she was horrified and in shame left the Earth and descended into the world of darkness and death below. She became known as Hine-nui-te-Po, the goddess of death.

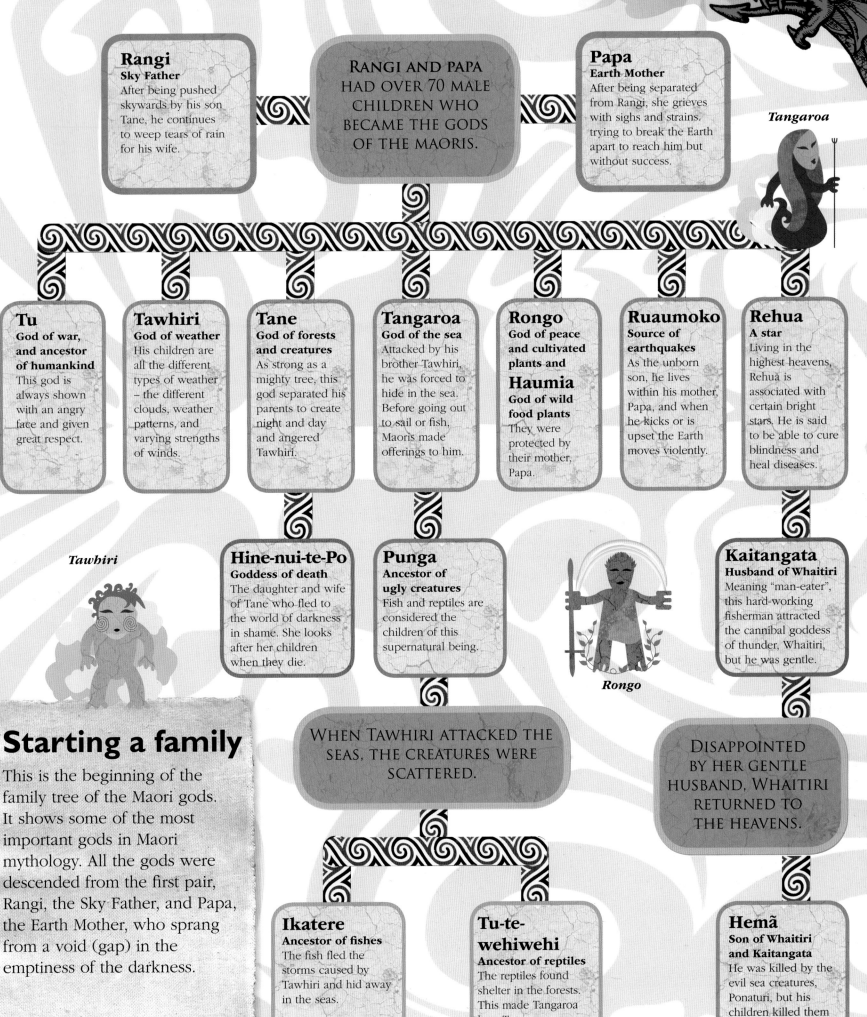

Rangi
Sky Father
After being pushed skywards by his son Tane, he continues to weep tears of rain for his wife.

RANGI AND PAPA HAD OVER 70 MALE CHILDREN WHO BECAME THE GODS OF THE MAORIS.

Papa
Earth Mother
After being separated from Rangi, she grieves with sighs and strains, trying to break the Earth apart to reach him but without success.

Tangaroa

Tu
God of war, and ancestor of humankind
This god is always shown with an angry face and given great respect.

Tawhiri
God of weather
His children are all the different types of weather – the different clouds, weather patterns, and varying strengths of winds.

Tane
God of forests and creatures
As strong as a mighty tree, this god separated his parents to create night and day and angered Tawhiri.

Tangaroa
God of the sea
Attacked by his brother Tawhiri, he was forced to hide in the sea. Before going out to sail or fish, Maoris made offerings to him.

Rongo
God of peace and cultivated plants and
Haumia
God of wild food plants
They were protected by their mother, Papa.

Ruaumoko
Source of earthquakes
As the unborn son, he lives within his mother, Papa, and when he kicks or is upset the Earth moves violently.

Rehua
A star
Living in the highest heavens, Rehua is associated with certain bright stars. He is said to be able to cure blindness and heal diseases.

Tawhiri

Hine-nui-te-Po
Goddess of death
The daughter and wife of Tane who fled to the world of darkness in shame. She looks after her children when they die.

Punga
Ancestor of ugly creatures
Fish and reptiles are considered the children of this supernatural being.

Kaitangata
Husband of Whaitiri
Meaning "man-eater", this hard-working fisherman attracted the cannibal goddess of thunder, Whaitiri, but he was gentle.

Rongo

Starting a family

This is the beginning of the family tree of the Maori gods. It shows some of the most important gods in Maori mythology. All the gods were descended from the first pair, Rangi, the Sky Father, and Papa, the Earth Mother, who sprang from a void (gap) in the emptiness of the darkness.

WHEN TAWHIRI ATTACKED THE SEAS, THE CREATURES WERE SCATTERED.

DISAPPOINTED BY HER GENTLE HUSBAND, WHAITIRI RETURNED TO THE HEAVENS.

Ikatere
Ancestor of fishes
The fish fled the storms caused by Tawhiri and hid away in the seas.

Tu-te-wehiwehi
Ancestor of reptiles
The reptiles found shelter in the forests. This made Tangaroa hate Tane.

Hemã
Son of Whaitiri and Kaitangata
He was killed by the evil sea creatures, Ponaturi, but his children killed them in revenge.

Biography
Maui, demi-god and hero

Family connections
Maui's mother was Taranga, guardian of the path to the underworld and his father was Makea-Tutura, a chief of the underworld. In some versions of the story, his wife is Hina, goddess of the Moon, death, and rebirth.

Childhood story
Maui was born early, so he was weak and very small. Thinking he wouldn't survive, his mother wrapped him up and threw him into the ocean. Sea creatures found and cared for him, and carried him safely to a beach, where Rangi, the Sky Father, brought him up. When he was older, Maui returned to his mother's village, rejoined her and his four brothers (who became jealous of him), and found his father.

Maui, the tiny trickster

Well-known throughout Polynesia, Maui is a **demi-god** with magical powers that he uses to carry out his **scheming** plans. Despite his small size, many myths describe his astounding feats, like increasing the amount of sunlight in a day, and creating an island. During his life, he broke rules, lied and cheated, playing **tricks** to achieve his ambitions. In the end though, he died trying to eliminate death for all people.

Slowing the Sun

Maui's mother wove cloth out of bark, but there were never enough daylight hours for her bark to dry. To solve the problem, Maui made a plan – using coconut fibre, he wove a strong rope. With the help of his brothers, he captured the Sun as it was rising, and beat it. The Sun pleaded with him to stop, and promised to move more slowly across the sky. Maui agreed, and the Sun kept its promise, so from then on, the days were much longer.

In order to follow his mother down to the underworld to meet his father, Maui turned himself into a wood pigeon.

In this painting, Maui transformed himself into a lizard to crawl inside the body of Hine-nui-te-Po (see page 22).

Defying death

Maui believed he could achieve immortality for humans by crawling through the body of Hine-nui-te-Po, goddess of death. As she lay sleeping, he transformed himself into a lizard (or caterpillar), and began inching into her. A bird, excited by the sight, chirped, and woke Hine-nui-te-Po. She realized she was being tricked, and crushed Maui to death between her thighs.

Bumper catch

On a fishing trip with his brothers, Maui used a magical hook that caught on the gable of a carved house sitting on the ocean floor. As his brothers rowed, Maui lifted up not only the house, but also a big chunk of land shaped like a fish. The Maori believe that this land was the North Island of New Zealand – they call it Te Ika a Maui, "The Fish of Maui".

Sedna and the trickster raven

Arctic spirits

God dolls

The Nenets, nomadic reindeer herders of Siberia, have lots of gods, each one represented by a doll-like figure. All these are carried in a sacred sledge, which is regularly anointed with reindeer blood. One figure, the "old woman of the chum" (reindeer-skin home), has her own sleeping place in each family tent. When her help is needed, she's fed with blood and vodka.

Waste world

For the Chukchi, who live in Siberia too, Raven is also responsible for creating the world – in the traditional story, he ejected it from the sky as poo. Modern versions (made more acceptable) often describe how Raven dropped the world from on high as a big rock.

Daughter of the Sun

The Sami tribe of Scandinavia worships many gods and goddesses. Among them is Aknidi, daughter of the Sun. The tribe believes that she once lived among humans, teaching them songs and stories, and passing on skills. But people were jealous of her wisdom and beauty, and crushed her under a rock. Now, she lives permanently in the sky.

The sea dominates the lives of all *Arctic peoples* – traditionally, the animals that live there provide food, clothing, skins to make tents, bone to make tools, and even oil for lamps. For them, the sea is ruled by the goddess *Sedna*, and the story of how she became a goddess is a popular myth, with many different versions.

Sedna was a beautiful girl who lived with her father. They were a happy family, but a poor one. But Sedna was very vain – she spent hours looking at her reflection in the water, and combing her long black hair. Many men asked to marry her, but she refused them all. Finally, her father pleaded, "Please, we have hardly any food, and soon we will starve. You need a husband to take care of you – you must marry the next man who asks". But Sedna ignored him, and went on combing her hair.

Soon after, a strange hunter approached their camp. His face was covered against the cold, but he was dressed in fur, and he looked prosperous. Sedna's father approached him. "Sir, if you are looking for a wife, come and meet my beautiful daughter – she will be perfect." The hunter promised to provide her with plentiful food and rich clothing, and the deal was done. Sedna, protesting loudly, was carried to his kayak for the journey to his home.

After a long time, they arrived at an island. Sedna looked around, but she could see no house and no tent – just rocks and cliffs. The hunter uncovered his head and laughed – he was not a man, but an evil raven in disguise, and the girl's home was a clump of animal hair and feathers on the hard rock. The raven was cruel to Sedna, and gave her no delicious meat to eat – only raw fish, brought to her in his raven's beak. Day after day, the young girl sat on the windy rock and howled in misery and fear. Eventually, through the Arctic winds, Sedna's father heard her cry, and knew that he had caused her pain. He set out to find her, and after a long, cold journey, he finally found her island. As soon as she saw him, she jumped in his kayak and they paddled away.

Soon, Sedna noticed a black speck in the sky. She was terrified – she knew it was the raven, come to claim her. When it came near, her father beat it off with his paddle, but the evil animal flapped his wings on the water, and whipped up a vicious storm. The tiny kayak dipped and dived in the huge waves until Sedna's father, terrified, tossed her out and screamed at the raven, "Take her back – leave me alone!".

The desperate girl screamed and struggled and tried to hold on to the boat, but her father had lost all reason. He took his knife, and cut off her fingers, one by one. As they fell into the ocean, they turned into creatures – fish, seals, otters, and whales. Finally, Sedna's body sank to the ocean floor, but she did not die. She became the goddess of the sea, with the head and body of a woman, and the tail of a fish. (This description closely resembles that of European mermaids – hair combing is often mentioned in these sightings too).

For ever after, it was Sedna's fury that churned up violent storms. And when hunters couldn't find food for their families, it was because she kept her creatures close to her.

Keeping Sedna happy
When food was scarce, a shaman swam under the sea and calmed Sedna by combing her hair (she had no fingers to do this). Then, she allowed hunters to catch plenty of sea creatures. Even now, when a hunter kills a seal, he drops water in its mouth to thank Sedna for her generosity.

Kaang and the world tree

San people paintings from South Africa are thousands of years old.

Kaang, creator god
Family connections
Kaang, also known as /Kaggen, Cagn, Kho, Thora, and Kang, is a creator god; the god of nature. In /Xam San mythology (a branch of the San people) Kaang is /Kaggen the Mantis and his wife is the Dassie (the rock rabbit), the Mother of Bees. Their adopted daughter is the Porcupine and she is married to /Kwammang-a (a meerkat).

Ancient nation
Stories about Kaang originated from the San people (bushmen) of the Kalahari Desert. They are thought to be one of the oldest nations in the world with a history going back 20,000 years. Thousands of years ago, they migrated south from northern Africa and their stories spread.

Spiritual connection
The San have a deep connection with nature and believe every living thing has a spirit.

The Lord of death
Kaang's enemy is Gauna, Lord of Death. Kaang taught the people laws and rituals to stop Gauna's ghosts rising from their graves and invading the world. When the people ignored Kaang he moved to the sky, taking the secret of immortality with him. Since then, people have been preyed on by the Lord of death.

Kaang is said to visit his people in the form of a praying mantis.

Once upon a time, people and animals lived peacefully together under the surface of the world. There was no Sun, but they had **light**, they were warm, and they had everything they needed. The creatures and people understood each other and lived **happily** side by side.

One day Kaang, the creator god, decided to build another world. He made a huge, magnificent tree with branches that spread over the whole countryside and he filled the branches with the most wonderful things. Then he dug a hole down to where the humans and animals lived. Taking a man by the hand, he led him up the passageway he had made into the world above.

They sat down by the hole and soon a woman appeared at its entrance. She explored the world with the man and they were overjoyed with all they saw. They called down the hole for the others to join them and with the giraffe leading the way, all the people and animals came up into the new world. The birds flew in the top of the branches, excited by all that they saw. The other animals looked around and were very content.

Kaang called them all together and explained the laws of the new world. He told them to live in peace and harmony and to listen to one another, but he also warned them not to make fire as it would bring great evil into the world.

The people promised faithfully to follow
the new laws. Kaang left them and went to
a place where he could watch them secretly.
All went well until the Sun began
to set. It got colder and colder and darker
and darker until the Sun disappeared
completely. The people began to worry.
They could not see as well as the animals, and they
were cold because they did not have fur or feathers
to keep them warm. Where had the Sun gone?
Was it ever going to come back? Were they stuck
in this dark, cold world forever?

As their worry turned to fear and their fear
turned to panic, one man suddenly shouted that they
must make fire. Fire would give them the light and
warmth that they wanted and it would help them
survive. The other people quickly agreed
and as soon as the fire was lit, they huddled
around it, comforted by its
flames and warmed by its heat.
They turned happily to their
friends, the animals, but they were
no-where to be seen; they had
run away and hidden, terrified of the fire's flames.

"Come back!" shouted the people, but the
animals could no longer understand them and only
heard yelling, which made them run away again.

Suddenly the people remembered their
promise to Kaang and fell silent. They had broken
their promise, and in doing so had broken the
special relationship they'd had with their friends,
the animals, forever.

The first people

Many world myths tell how the gods took several attempts at creating the **perfect race** at the start of time, moulding people from familiar objects, such as wood and clay. Others tell of just one race of people and their **journeys** from one world to another, searching for the perfect home.

◀ **Ask and Embla,** **Norse** The gods created an area for humans to live called Midgard *(see page 90)* and surrounded it with the giant Ymir's eyebrows. The man, Ask, was made from a fallen ash tree and the woman, Embla, was made from a fallen elm. Odin breathed life into them, Vili gave them thoughts and feelings, and Ve gave them sight and hearing.

▲ **Coyote,** **North America** The Coyote features as a creator god in many native American legends. The Coast Miwok nation tell how Coyote made people out of turkey, buzzard, raven, and crow feathers.

▲ **Creator gods,** **Mayas** The ancient Mayan text, the *Popol Vuh* describes how the creator gods first made animals but these did not worship them. Then they made creatures made of clay, but they too turned away from the gods. The third race was carved from wood but the gods destroyed them in a flood. The fourth and final race were created from maize dough.

▲ **Spider woman, North America** Several native American nations, including the Hopi, the Navajo, and Cherokee have legends of the spider woman helping humankind move from one world to another.

◀ **Tiki, Polynesia** In some myths, Tane, the god of the birds and the forests, created man – Tiki first, then woman. Others say that Tiki created the first human by mixing clay with his blood.

SEEING THINGS
For more about Polynesian gods see page 22.

▲ **Khnum, Ancient Egypt** It was said in ancient Egypt that the creator of humankind and god of the River Nile moulded children out of river clay and placed them inside the wombs of women.

◀ **Nu Gua, China** The goddess Nu Gua made the first people out of clay because she was lonely. However, she noticed that her creations grew old and died, and, as she didn't want to go on creating new ones forever, she gave them the ability to have children.

▲ **Prometheus, Ancient Greece** Zeus gave Prometheus the job of making people from mud and his brother Epimetheus the task of giving them useful qualities. Unfortunately, by the time Epimetheus had finished dealing with the other animals, he didn't have anything useful to give humans, so Prometheus gave people the ability to walk upright and make fire *(see page 34)*.

Ancient Greek gods

Ancient Greeks believed there were **immortal** gods and goddesses who took an interest in people's everyday lives and had emotions just like humans. They were a family of powerful giants called **Titans** who roamed the heavens and Earth. Zeus became their king and lived with his wife and children on **Mount Olympus**, the highest mountain in Greece.

Gaia (Tellus)
Mother Earth
She was born out of the chaos at the beginning of creation. She married Uranus, her first son.

URANUS AND GAIA HAD TWELVE CHILDREN KNOWN AS THE TITANS. CRONUS AND RHEA WERE TWO OF THEM.

Cronus (Saturn)
God of Time
Although the youngest of the Titans, he became the ruler of the heavens when he killed his father.

Rhea (Cybele)
Mother of the gods
She protected her son Zeus from being eaten by Cronus, who had devoured their other children.

Demeter (Ceres)
Goddess of agriculture
She taught people how to sow and plough and was often shown with some corn.

Hera (Juno)
Goddess of marriage
She often tried to punish Zeus's other women and their children.

Zeus (Jupiter)
God of heavens and Earth
He killed Cronus and took over as ruler. He sent thunderbolts against his enemies.

Poseidon (Neptune)
God of the seas
He lived on the ocean floor in a palace made of coral and gems. If angry, he caused stormy seas.

HERA AND ZEUS HAD FOUR CHILDREN, ARES, HEBE, HEPHAESTUS, AND EILEITHYIA.

ZEUS HAD LOTS OF CHILDREN WITH VARIOUS OTHER WOMEN, WHICH MADE HERA JEALOUS.

Ares (Mars)
God of war
He was cruel and violent and was not liked by the other gods. He was sometimes shown with a vulture.

Hebe (Juventas)
Goddess of youth
She was the cupbearer of nectar and ambrosia, which the gods drank to stay immortal.

Hephaestus (Vulcan)
God of the blacksmith's fire
He was the patron of craftsmen and shown wielding an axe or a blacksmith's hammer.

Uranus (Caelus)
Father Sky
He hated his children, which included the Titans, Cyclops, and other Giants.

Battle of the Titans
Zeus led the terrifying battle against his father, Cronus, and the other Titans to win control as the ruler of the heavens. His mother and brothers and sisters and some of the Giants helped him.

An ancient Greek frieze showing the battle between the gods and the Giants.

WHEN **CRONUS** CUT **URANUS** INTO PIECES, **APHRODITE** SPRANG UP WHERE THE DROPS OF HIS BLOOD FELL INTO THE SEA.

Greek to Latin
The Romans worshipped many of the ancient Greek gods and goddesses, but gave them Latin names. These have been written in brackets. The Romans gave them the same characteristics and added to the many myths about them.

Aphrodite (Venus)
Goddess of love and beauty
She was often shown with a sceptre, myrtle, and a dove. She was the wife of Hephaestus.

Hades (Pluto)
God of the underworld
He ruled the land of the dead. He had a helmet that made the wearer invisible.

Hestia (Vesta)
Goddess of the home
She gave up her seat on Mount Olympus to look after the fire within the mountain.

Apollo (Apollo)
God of light, music, and healing
He was musical and poetical, and a keen hunter, and features in many myths about his lovers.

Hermes (Mercury)
God of trade and protector of travellers He carried messages from the gods and held a caduceus (winged staff) and wore winged boots and helmet.

Athena (Minerva)
Goddess of wisdom and war
She sprang fully armed from Zeus's head. Her symbols were an owl and an olive tree.

Artemis (Diana)
Goddess of the Moon and wild animals She would roam the mountain forests with the nymphs and her wild animals.

Dionysus (Bacchus)
God of wine and feasting
He could be either joyful and festive or brutal and angry. He was said to have invented wine.

33

Prometheus
The Titans
Prometheus was a Titan, a race of giants created by the sky god Uranus and the Earth goddess Gaia (see page 32). His parents were two Titans, Iapetus and Themis and his brothers were Atlas, Epimetheus, and Menoetius.

Prometheus married Pronoia and they had a son called Deucalion. Deucalion married Pyrrha, the daughter of Epimetheus and Pandora, the first woman.

What's in a name?
Prometheus's name means "Forethought", while his brother's name, Epimetheus, means "Afterthought".

Fire for mankind
When Zeus, the ruler of the gods, hid fire from the people, Prometheus went up to the heavens to steal it. He hid the flame in the hollow stem of some fennel and brought it down to Earth.

Immortality
In one of the Greek myths, Prometheus became immortal after helping a centaur, Chiron. Chiron the centaur was shot by one of Heracles' poisoned arrows. He was in terrible pain and wanted to die but he couldn't because he was immortal. Prometheus took pity on Chiron and offered him his human right to die, thereby gaining Chiron's immortality for himself.

How evil came into the world

The people made regular sacrifices of meat to the gods, but Prometheus noticed that the gods always took all the best meat. Wanting to help the people he had made and unafraid of Zeus, he encouraged the people to play a trick on the gods.

First, the people prepared two packages. One was full of bones and wrapped in fat, the other contained meat, but was wrapped in animal gut. They took the offerings to Zeus, and, as expected, he chose the better-looking parcel covered in the fat.

Zeus returned to his palace. He unwrapped the offering and immediately flew into a terrible temper. How dare the people trick him! He was determined to get his revenge. Zeus finally decided to punish mankind by withholding from them the knowledge of fire. After all, he reasoned, they were inferior to the gods and incapable of using such great power wisely.

Prometheus, however, disagreed. Taking pity on mankind, he secretly stole some of the gods' fire and gave it to the people. He taught them how to use it to cook food and smelt metal to make weapons.

When Zeus found out, he was outraged. He decided to punish both Prometheus and the people for their deceiving and disobedient ways. Prometheus was bound in chains and tied to a rock on Mount Caucasus. Every day an eagle came and pecked out his liver and every night his liver was made whole again, ready for a new onslaught the following day. This continued, day and night, for thousands of years until Heracles shot the eagle with one of his poisoned arrows.

To punish mankind, the gods created the first woman.

Prometheus and the eagle on Mount Caucasus

In some of the retellings of this myth, Zeus's present is a box.

An alternative ending
In later retellings of this myth, Pandora's box contained all the good things in the world. When she opened the box, all the good things flew out and went back to the gods on Mount Olympus, leaving just the evils and Hope in the world.

The god Hephaestus made her from clay, Athena gave her the gift of life, Hermes taught her the art of persuasion and cunning, and Aphrodite gave her beauty. They named her Pandora, meaning "all gifts", and gave her to Epimetheus as his wife.

As Pandora left the gods, Zeus gave her one last present; a chest, tightly sealed. He warned her that it was hers to keep but she must never open it. Pandora was so curious to know what the chest contained that once she was living on Earth she couldn't resist opening it. As she lifted the lid, all the evils and diseases flew out and quickly spread around the world. In dismay, Pandora shut the lid, but by then just one small comfort remained behind; Hope.

35

Flood stories

In ancient mythology, floods are often sent by **vengeful** gods who wish to wipe the slate clean and begin again with **creation**. Some of the flood myths may have arisen from the discovery of seashell and fish **fossils** on mountainsides.

SEEING THINGS For more about Gilgamesh see page 126.

▲ **Utnapishtim,** **Mesopotamia** In the epic tale of Gilgamesh, there is a character called Utnapishtim, who is the survivor of a great flood. He was warned by a god that other gods planned to flood the world as there were too many people in it. Utnapishtim, his family, and his animals survived the seven-day storm by building an ark.

▲ **Navajo nation,** **North America** Navajo legends tell of several worlds that were created, one by one. The first people climbed up into the first world but were dissatisfied with it. They climbed up into another world, then another. The third world they visited was also an unhappy place. A great flood came and destroyed it, but the First Man built a mountain so that the people could escape.

◄ **Chalchiuhtlicue,** **Mexico** The Mexican goddess of rivers and lakes once flooded the whole world to get rid of all those who were evil, but those who were good were turned into fish and were saved.

▲ **Viracocha,** Incas The first people were drowned in a flood because of their evil ways. The creator god Viracocha formed another race of humans from stones. Disguised as a beggar, he travelled around teaching them how to live. When he saw that they were as evil as his first creations he cried.

▶ **Zeus,** Ancient Greece Zeus, angry with the third set of humans he had made, decided to destroy them in a flood. However Prometheus warned his son Deucalion and his son's wife Pyrrha and they escaped the deluge in a wooden chest.

▲ **Vishnu,** India
King Manu was washing in a river when a fish swam into his hands and asked to be saved. Manu kept the fish, which grew bigger and bigger until it finally revealed itself to be the god Vishnu. He warned Manu of a great flood and helped him escape in a boat containing seeds, medicinal herbs, animals, and some wise men.

◀ **Noah,** Middle
East The story of Noah and the Great Flood occurs in Jewish, Islamic, and Christian scripture. The 40-day flood was a punishment for people's ungodly behaviour. God saved Noah in an ark as he was the only righteous man left on Earth. God promised after the flood that he would never again destroy living creatures.

Mexican gods

Family connections
Ometeotl was the first god in Aztec myths. He existed as the male Ometecuhtli and the female Omecihuatl. They had four offspring, known as the four Tezcatlipocas: Huitzilopochtli, the Sun god; Quetzalcoatl, god of the wind; Tezcatlipoca, the dark mirror god; and Xipe-Totec, the fertility god.

What's in a name?
Quetzal is the name of a bird with green feathers found in Central America, though the word is sometimes used to mean "feathered" or "precious". Coatl means "snake" but it can also mean "twin".

Mexico's creator god
The feathered-snake god Quetzalcoatl was worshipped for thousands of years in Mexico. Temple sculptures from the Olmec civilization are 3,500 years old. The Mayan civilization in southern Mexico worshipped a very similar snake-bird called Kukulkan.

Legendary ruler
It is thought that the god Quetzalcoatl might have been a real ruler called Topiltzin, a ruler of the Toltec civilization.

Aztec King Moctezuma exchanging gifts with Cortés.

The arrival of the Spanish
When the Spanish arrived in Mexico for the first time, the Aztec ruler enthusiastically welcomed their leader, Hernán Cortés, thinking that he was Quetzalcoatl who had returned to save his people.

Quetzalcoatl and Tezcatlipoca

After creating four worlds, one after another, the creator god Quetzalcoatl was happy with the fifth world he had made. He turned himself into a man and went to the Toltec city of Tula where he became emperor priest of the people. He was a **good** and able ruler and taught his people many things; how to grow corn, weave, write, make music, dance, and create art. He banned human sacrifice and **ruled wisely**, setting just laws for the people to live by.

However, Quetzalcoatl was not the only god. There was also an evil god, Quetzalcoatl's brother Tezcatlipoca. He despised Quetzalcoatl and his just ways and was jealous of his power over the people. So, he came up with a plan to trick Quetzalcoatl into stepping down as the people's leader.

Quetzalcoatl, the good creator god, is often depicted with feathers and snakes.

One day, he visited Quetzalcoatl in disguise as an old man and gave him a special gift of a magical potion. He urged Quetzalcoatl to drink the potion saying it would make him feel young and give him renewed energy. Quetzalcoatl drank the potion, not realizing it was in fact just ordinary alcohol. After a while he became quite drunk and witless.

Tezcatlipoca took advantage of Quetzalcoatl's befuddled state and taking a picture of himself showed it to Quetzalcoatl, telling him it was a mirror. Quetzalcoatl was horrified to see that he looked so old and frail. In shock, he stood by helpless as Tezcatlipoca destroyed the gifts that Quetzalcoatl had given his people; all the corn, the music, and their art, and finally all the people.

Good versus evil
The eternal struggle between good and evil forces is a recurring theme in myths around the world. In the Middle East, there are stories of the struggle between the creator of life Spenta Mainyu (Ahura Mazda) and the destroyer Angra Mainyu; in North America the Iroquois, Mohawk, and Huron nations tell of good and evil creator twins in continual battle with each other.

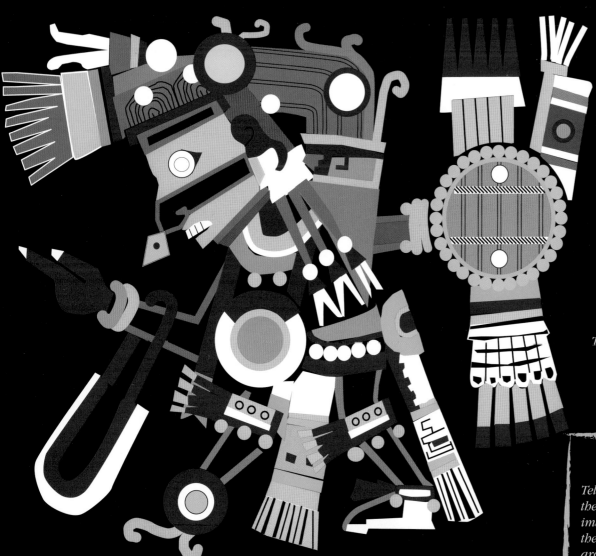

The evil god Tezcatlipoca

PERFORM A PUPPET SHOW
Tell the story in your own words with these colourful stick puppets. Trace the images and colour them in. Then stick the tracing paper onto card and cut around the shapes. Tape your puppets onto sticks and you're ready to go!

Once Quetzalcoatl had sobered up, he burned his palace and ordered the birds to leave the land. Then he made a raft of snakes and set himself adrift on the Atlantic Ocean. As he drifted towards the Sun his body was destroyed by fire. His heart rose up to become the planet Venus, the morning star.

Tezcatlipoca had finally got his wish and destroyed his brother. However, before Quetzalcoatl left, he vowed that one day he would return and rule over a peaceful and contented kingdom.

Egyptian gods

The ancient Egyptians had over 2,000 gods, some that were worshipped throughout the country and others with just a local following. The Egyptians lived in **terror** of evil spirits and feared the displeasure of the gods. They thought that the gods ruled over and affected **every aspect** of their lives.

The first pharoah

The people of ancient Egypt believed that their rulers, such as Narmer (above), were half man half god, and were direct descendants of Ra. Ra took on the shape of a man and became the first pharaoh. Isis then tricked him into passing her the secret Name of Power. With this, her son Horus became the living pharaoh and her husband Osiris the dead pharaoh ruling over the underworld.

Atum-Ra
God of the Sun

He was the first being to emerge from the vast motionless waters of Nun in the beginning, Atum-Ra was the creator god, who created and named all things.

ATUM SPAT OUT THE ELEMENTS OF MOISTURE, HIS DAUGHTER TEFNUT, AND AIR, HIS SON SHU.

Tefnut
Goddess of rain

She was said to have caused the terrible weather that devastated Egypt in 2200 BCE because she argued with Shu and left the country. She changed into a cat, destroying anyone who came near and was often shown with the head of a lioness.

Nut
Goddess of sky and stars

This goddess was linked with protecting the dead after they entered the afterlife. She was sometimes shown as a sycamore tree as this was the wood that coffins were made from. Other images show her bent over in an arch and covered in stars, separating chaos above and the ordered universe below.

THE TWINS MARRIED EACH OTHER AND HAD TWO CHILDREN CALLED GEB AND NUT.

Shu
God of air

He was said to bring the Sun to life every morning. He and Tefnut were worshipped in lion form, and people slept with lion headrests to make sure they woke up the next morning, like the Sun. Shu also held up the sky.

Geb God of the Earth

He was shown lying on the ground with one arm and knee in the air, representing the hills and the valleys. The ancient Egyptians believed that earthquakes were caused by him laughing.

His body was coloured in the black of the fertile mud along the banks of the river Nile.

GEB AND NUT HAD FOUR CHILDREN, OSIRIS, ISIS, NEPHTHYS AND SETH.

Seth
God of violence and the desert (foreign lands)
This powerful god was associated with the colour red, as this had a similar Egyptian word to desert. He killed his brother to seize control of Egypt.

His head was of an unknown creature.

Nephthys
Goddess of divine assistance and protection
She was the comforter of those who mourned and accompanied the dead on the nightboat to the underworld.

She was sometimes shown with outstretched hawk's wings as a symbol of protection.

Osiris
God of the dead
He was killed by his brother Seth and his 14 scattered body pieces were collected by Isis and rejoined by her magic.

He was the form of the dead pharaohs and was shown as a mummy, holding a crook and a flail and wearing the Egyptian crown.

Isis
Goddess of magic and life
As a loving wife to Osiris and devoted mother to Horus, this goddess with magical powers was one of the greatest and most popular of all the gods.

A throne was the symbol of her name.

Anubis God of embalming
He was at first the god of the dead but then replaced by Osiris and became the guide to the dead on the path to the underworld.

He had the head of a jackal, a dog-like animal that hung around cemeteries, lurking in the dark shadows.

OSIRIS WAS SEDUCED BY NEPHTHYS AND THEY HAD ONE CHILD, ANUBIS.

ISIS AND OSIRIS MARRIED AND HAD ONE CHILD HORUS.

Horus
God of the sky, war, and protection
Each new Egyptian pharaoh was considered to be another form of the god Horus. He was shown as a falcon, wearing a crown.

One of his eyes was the Sun and the other was the Moon, as it was weakened during his fight with Seth.

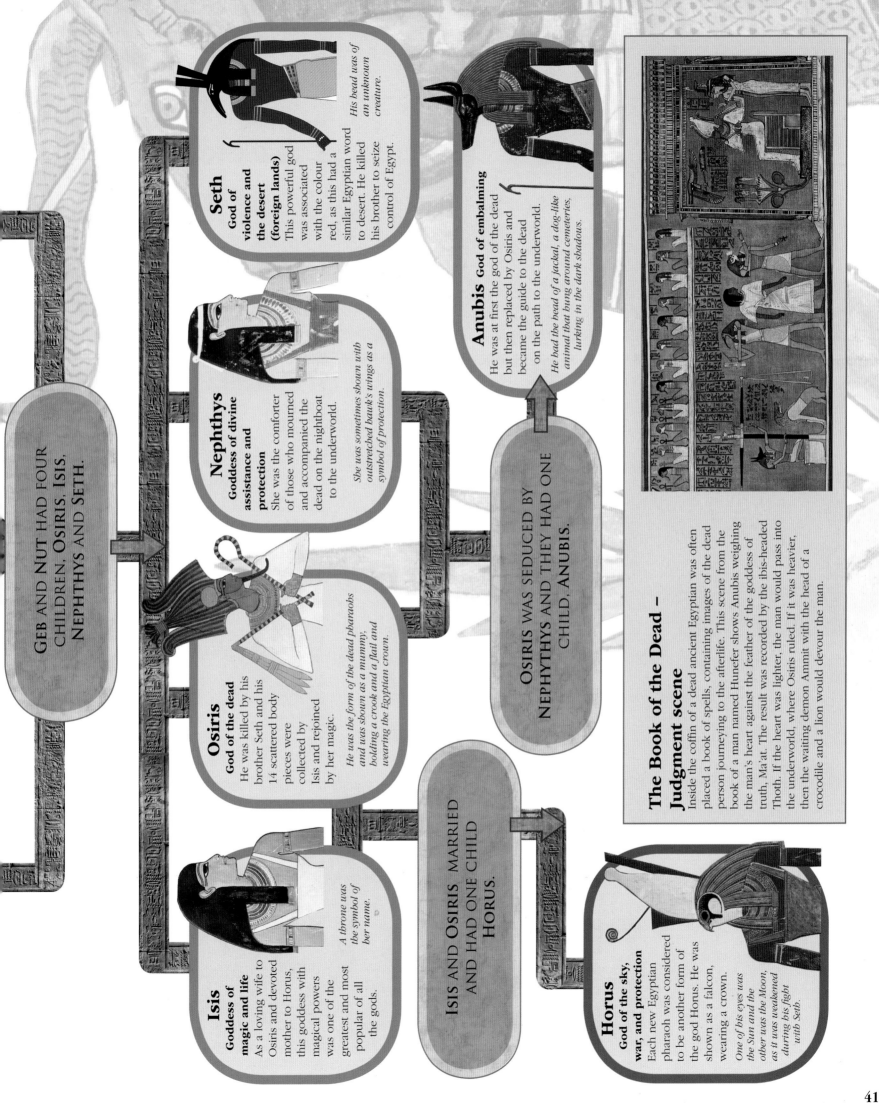

The Book of the Dead – Judgment scene
Inside the coffin of a dead ancient Egyptian was often placed a book of spells, containing images of the dead person journeying to the afterlife. This scene from the book of a man named Hunefer shows Anubis weighing the man's heart against the feather of the goddess of truth, Ma'at. The result was recorded by the ibis-headed Thoth. If the heart was lighter, the man would pass into the underworld, where Osiris ruled. If it was heavier, then the waiting demon Ammit with the head of a crocodile and a lion would devour the man.

Persephone
Goddess of springtime
Persephone (known as Proserpina in Roman myths) is daughter of Demeter, the goddess of agriculture, and Zeus. She was worshipped as the Greek goddess of spring, as well as queen of the underworld. Her Greek name means "to cause death" and her Roman one means "to spring forth".

Superstition
After she came back from the dead it was considered unlucky to say her name, so she was simply called Kore, which means "maiden".

Persephone holds a pomegranate, symbolizing her bond in marriage to Hades.

Demeter
Goddess of agriculture
Demeter (known to the Romans as Ceres) is often shown with a veil over her face and holding a goat's horn containing sheaves of grain – a cornucopia, or "horn of plenty" (see page 32). Sometimes she also holds a torch, a symbol of her vigilance in searching for her daughter. She is thought to hold the secret of immortality.

Nymphs
Becoming a siren
According to Ovid, a Roman poet, Demeter was furious with the nymphs for not saving her daughter. She turned them into bird women called sirens and sent them to search for her. As they flew, they sang, calling on Persephone to return.

A tale of four seasons

The Greek goddess Demeter had a daughter called Persephone. She was a **beautiful maiden**, with hair as gold as the ripening corn and skin as pale as the moonlight. Her beauty attracted many of the Olympian gods until Demeter hid her daughter away.

One day, Persephone was playing with some nymphs in a field when a crack suddenly appeared in the ground and a dark, terrifying character appeared riding on a chariot. Unknown to Persephone and Demeter, Zeus had promised his daughter to Hades, king of the underworld, and he had come to claim Persephone as his bride. Before Persephone could run away, Hades seized her and carried her off to his dark palace deep under the ground.

When Demeter heard that her daughter had been kidnapped she was beside herself with grief. She searched frantically for her lost daughter and was so distressed that she forgot her duties as goddess of corn and all growing things. The corn in the fields withered and died and the land took on a parched and barren look. Eventually the Sun took pity on her and told her that Hades had taken her. Demeter collapsed, veiling her face and weeping.

Zeus, alarmed at what was happening to the land, sent Hermes to the underworld to bring Persephone back. As long as she hadn't eaten anything she would be able to leave freely.

Cunningly Hades agreed to let Persephone go, but first gave her a pomegranate to eat. It looked so tempting that Persephone could not resist tasting it. As soon as she started to eat it, Hades revealed that she was now bound to the underworld forever. She could go and be with her mother for eight months, but had to return to Hades and take up her role as queen of the underworld for the last part of the year.

While Persephone was above the ground with her mother the world was beautiful and green, but on her return underground, Demeter stopped tending to the plants and did not allow any to grow. This is how the seasons of autumn and winter and the growing seasons came about.

Persephone is reunited for the spring and summer with her mother Demeter until each autumn and winter, when she must return to her husband Hades (Pluto).

Reason for the season

Many cultures have myths in which a god returns each year from the underworld and then descends again, coinciding with the cycle of the seasons. In ancient Mesopotamia, the shepherd-god Dumuzi (Tammuz) had to stay in the underworld so that his wife, Inanna (Ishtar – *see page 45*), could go back home. Dumuzi's sister took his place for six months of the year so he could spend time with Inanna on Earth.

When Inanna is on Earth without her husband it is autumn and winter. When he returns to her, spring and summer follow.

The underworld

Below the land of the living lies the **underworld**, where **souls** go when they die. In some cultures, it is a place where life came from and where it naturally returns, but others see it as a place of **punishment** for wrongdoing. Gods rule over these dark places and guards with supernatural abilities patrol the entrance.

▲ **Yama,** **South-east Asia** The god of death pulled a sinner's soul from his body with a rope. Depending on their sins, he judged whether the soul went to a place of happiness or to one of the many hells.

▲ **Apophis (Apep),** **Ancient Egypt**
The dead were buried with spells to protect their souls from Apophis, the god of chaos – a snake locked up in the Duat, the underworld. The Sun god Ra in the form of a cat killed the snake each night to prevent chaos from destroying the Sun and the world.

◄ **Cerberus,** **Ancient Greece** The snarling three-headed guard dog belonged to Hades, ruler of the underworld *(see pages 42–43)*. He patrolled the gates of Hades to stop any souls that tried to escape.

◀ Kurnugi,
Babylon (present-day Iraq) The underworld, Kurnugi, housed the winged souls of the dead and pale, blood-drinking Akhkharus. These demons attacked the goddess Ishtar *(see page 43)* when she visited her sister Ereshkigal, ruler of the underworld.

▶ Mictlantecuhtli,
Aztecs The god of death lived in Mictlan, the lowest part of the land of the dead. Souls who failed to enter paradise had to travel through nine hells to reach it, past python trees, giant alligators, and snakes.

▶ **Tartarus,** Ancient Greece
Those souls who had committed terrible sins were sent to the lowest part of the underworld, Tartarus, to receive a punishment that fitted their crimes. King Ixion was chained to an ever-spinning burning wheel for setting fire to his father-in-law and angering Zeus.

▶ P'an Kuan,
China As a gatekeeper and judge of the underworld, P'an Kuan recorded each soul's past behaviour and advised the great Lord of the Underworld Yen-lo on what their reward or punishment should be.

Magic and mayhem

People wanted to be able to explain the unexplainable and understand why good and bad things happened. Were there supernatural beings, mystical creatures, and mythical gods, protecting or harming, spreading fear, and causing misfortune?

The etching A Witch at her Cauldron *by Jan van de Velde, created in 1626.*

A *tall* story

The **towering** figure of the giant is found in myths from all corners of the world. Representing **strength**, the wild Earth, and fear, giants are a tall challenge for any hero to overcome.

▶ **Rübezahl,**
Germany European travellers feared the "Hey-Hey" men of the forest. Their echoing cries would make travellers lose their way and if the traveller mocked them he could end up losing his life. In Germany, the Hey-Hey shapechanger Rübezahl was sometimes called Lord of the Mountains.

▲ **Bran the Blessed,** **Wales** A good giant and King of Wales, Bran saved Wales from an Irish invasion after his sister's failed marriage to the King of Ireland. His preserved head entertained the seven warriors who survived the battle.

▲ **Polyphemus,** **Ancient Greece** This one-eyed giant (Cyclops) was a shepherd with a taste for humans. Polyphemus captured the Greek hero Odysseus, who outwitted and escaped the Cyclops by blinding him with a stake.

▲ **Hiranyakashipu,** **India** This scary-looking giant demon was one of the daityas – giants who craved the power of the Devas, the Hindu gods *(see page 98)*.

◄ Ymir,

Norse Ymir, founder of the Frost Giants, was killed at the hands of Odin and his brothers. They used his body to create Midgard (the Earth). His flesh was turned into soil, his blood became rivers and lakes, trees sprouted from his hair, and his bones formed mountains.

▶ Jack's Giant,

England "Fee-Fi-Foe-Fum! I smell the blood of an Englishman". The famous stories of Jack the giant killer and a people-eating giant have similarities to giant myths from Wales, France, and Scandinavia.

▲ Trolls, Scandinavia Tales are told of ugly, hairy, violent trolls, living in caves on remote mountainsides. Large stone landmarks in Scandinavia are said to be trolls that turned to stone when they came out into the sunlight.

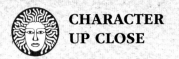
Biography
Circe, an enchantress

Family connections
She was the daughter of Helios, the god of the Sun, and Perse, who was one of 3,000 water nymphs. She was sister of Aeetes, the keeper of the Golden Fleece (see page 114), Perses, the King of Colchis, and Pasiphae, the wife of King Minos and the mother of the Minotaur (see page 108).

Children
One of her sons was Telegonus, who went in search of his father Odysseus and by mistake ended up killing him. He married Odysseus's wife, Penelope. Circe married one of Odysseus's sons, Telemachus, who went in search of his father.

An island home
Circe lived on the island of Aeaea, a mythical island, that may not have been an island but Mount Circeo, a headland off the west coast of Italy.

She lived in a grand palace, which stood in the middle of a clearing in a thick wood. Around the house roamed lions, bears, and wolves that were not dangerous because they had been drugged by her magic potions.

Passing the time
Her favourite pastime was to weave delicate and dazzling materials on her loom while singing beautifully.

Magic
Her magical powers included being able to darken the skies by moving the Moon or Sun, turn trees white, and move forests.

Circe could summon some powerful gods to help her with her magic, such as Nyx, the goddess of night, Chaos, the goddess of the air, and Hecate, another goddess of witchcraft.

Magical Circe

A **powerful sorceress**, Circe could transform her enemies into animals using magical **potions** and control nature with her magical **spells**. She is most famous for her role in the adventures of the hero, Odysseus, recounted in an epic poem by the ancient Greek poet, Homer.

Enchantment

In the epic poem, Odysseus and his crew arrived exhausted at Aeaea. After resting, the crew then went exploring and entered Circe's palace. She gave them a feast, but it was drugged with a potion that transformed them into pigs. Realizing his crew had vanished, Odysseus went to find them. On the way Hermes, the messenger god, met him. Hermes gave him a plant that would stop Circe's potion from working and also some useful advice that would charm Circe. It worked. Circe changed the crew back to men and they stayed on the island for over a year before continuing their journey.

She used herbs to create magical potions.

Tamed wild animals prowled around the palace and its grounds. They welcomed visitors with wagging tails.

Edmund Dulac
'11

Odysseus and the sirens

Circe lets Odysseus go, giving him advice on how to overcome the dangers that lay ahead.

Odysseus, the epic hero
Meet the family
Odysseus was known in Roman myths as Ulysses. His parents were the king and queen of Ithaca, Laertes and Anticlea. He became king when he grew up and married Penelope, cousin to Helen of Troy. They had a son, Telemachus.

A cunning hero
Odysseus displayed his heroic qualities in the Trojan War (see page 112), where he proved to be a skilful warrior.

An epic tale
The Odyssey is an epic poem written by the Greek poet Homer. It picks up the story of Odysseus after the Trojan War has ended and he is on his way home to his wife and son. Little does he know that this voyage will take him ten years. Many adventures follow, most of which are caused by the sea god Poseidon (Neptune) (see page 32), who is furious at Odysseus for blinding his son Polyphemus – a Cyclops (see page 48).

A long voyage
On his sea voyage, Odysseus and his twelve ships encountered storms, a land of drugged lotus eaters, a one-eyed, man-eating giant Cyclops, giant cannibals, and a witch-goddess, Circe (see page 50). These adventures cost Odysseus the loss of all but one of his ships and delayed him for many years.

While on Circe's island, Odysseus visited the blind prophet Tiresias in the underworld. Tiresias told him that further **dangers** lay ahead but he would die old and contented. Odysseus also met his mother's ghost. She warned him that his family and home were in danger.

After hearing news from home, Odysseus was keen to continue his voyage. Before he set sail, Circe warned him that first he had to pass the sirens, sea nymphs who lured sailors to their death by their sweet singing. Odysseus ordered his men to plug their ears with beeswax. However, wishing to hear the siren's song for himself, he made his men tie him to the ship's mast, with strict instructions not to untie him, no matter how earnestly he begged.

In this way, they sailed on. Odysseus had been wise to instruct his men as he had. The sirens' song was so temptingly beautiful that he couldn't resist their call.

Struggling to free himself, he cried out to be untied, but his sailors only tightened his bonds even more. Eventually they past the island and were safe.

Next, Odysseus's ship came to a narrow channel with tall cliffs on either side. A fearsome six-headed sea creature called Scylla lived on one side, while on the other side churned the great whirlpool of the monster Charybdis *(see page 61)*. Could they really escape the clutches of these terrifying monsters?

(see page 61)

DRAW A COMIC STRIP

Have a go at making your own comic strip of Odysseus's voyage. In each frame draw one of the stages of the story. Use bold colours to create an eye-catching tale and add speech bubbles to record Odysseus and the crew's reactions to each danger.

Ignoring Circe's advice to sail past them as fast as possible, Odysseus stood on deck to fight the monsters. By the time the ship had sailed through the channel, six sailors' lives had been lost.

Eventually Odysseus and his men landed on the island of Thrinacia. Odysseus warned his men not to touch the animals as they belonged to the Sun god Helios. However once he was asleep, the men ignored him and killed some oxen. As punishment, Zeus waited for them to set sail and then struck their ship with a thunderbolt; all but Odysseus drowned.

Deadly maidens
Nymphs who tempted people to an untimely fate appear in many of the world's myths. The legendary Lorelei on Germany's River Rhine were said to lure unwary sailors to their deaths. The mythical Huldra of Scandinavia had animal tails and lived in mountains and forests, ready to lure unsuspecting travellers to their death.

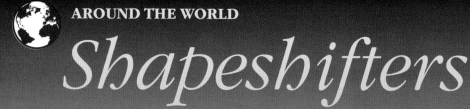

Shapeshifters

Shapeshifting is the **ability** of a being, whether it is a god, mortal, or animal, to **change** its form. This may be used to **trick** others or to enable them to live among humans, though some use it to hide too.

▶ **Ra (Khepri),**
Ancient Egypt
Ancient Egyptian gods were sometimes painted with animal heads to highlight a particular aspect of their character. Khepri, the dawning Sun, was likened to the scarab beetle; both seemed to appear from nowhere as if created from nothing.

▲ **La Fee Melusine, France** A beautiful fairy maiden, half woman half fish, married a human on condition that he did not look at her when she changed shape once a week. One day her husband spied on her and saw her fish tail. In dismay, Melusine fled, never to be seen again.

◀ **Nøkken, Scandinavia** These water spirits were said to transform themselves into beautiful white horses to capture people. As soon as humans tried to ride these horses, the Nøkken would leap back into the water and drown them.

SEEING THINGS
For more about water spirits see page 66.

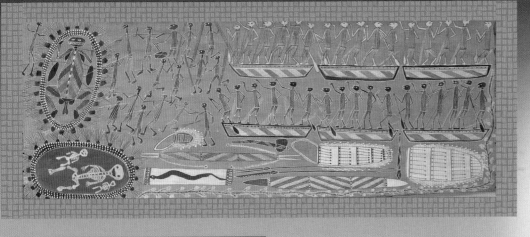

▲ Lumaluma, Australia A myth of the
Yolngu people of Northern Australia tells of a
whale that became human and travelled about
the land teaching sacred rituals. However he had
a huge appetite and claimed all the food that was
found was sacred and therefore for him alone.
The people eventually banded together and
killed him because of his greed.

◀ Proteus, Ancient Greece
Son of the Greek Titan Oceanus, Proteus
had the ability to predict the future, but
often turned into an animal to escape
people who wanted to pester him with
questions. Here Cyrene the water nymph
persuades him to reveal the future to
her by threatening him with a spear.

◀ Kitsune, Japan
Kitsunes are intelligent spirits
with magical powers. One myth
tells of a kitsune that fell in love
and married a man while in
human form. Her husband's dog
sensed she was not really a
human and continually attacked
her until she gave up pretending,
turned back into a fox, and fled.

▶ Selkie, Northern Europe
At a distance, seal heads in the sea look
like humans, which may have given rise
to myths about selkies; seals that shed
their skin and turn into humans. If a
selkie's sealskin was ever found, it
would transform back into a seal
and swim away. Accounts of
sealskin-clad Saami people visiting
from Norway may also have helped
create the selkie myth.

Biography
Werewolves

Characterisatics

Werewolves were humans who changed into a wolf during the night of a full Moon. They were said to be incredibly strong and possess superhuman senses. Legend had it that a person became a werewolf either by being bitten by one, because a curse had been put on them, or because they had been born that way.

The vampire link

Some myths from ancient Greece and the Slavic nations of Eastern Europe tell of werewolves that turned into vampires when they died. They wandered around on moonlit nights, in the shape of a person or animal, and fed on the blood of animals and people.

That's madness

"Lycanthropy" is a name given to a disease of mind and body, where people believe they have been, or are, an animal of some kind. People often believe they are a wolf or some other ferocious animal, such as a tiger. There are records of this disease existing in Europe, northern Asia, Africa, and India.

Dog-headed race

Marco Polo and other explorers in the Middle Ages told of a cruel race of dog-headed men, called Cynocephali, who lived in India and Africa and who ate people. Some thought these were werewolves, others that they were the first ever sightings of baboons.

Werewolves

Several hundred years ago, **wolves** were a common sight in the European countryside at dusk. With their human-like howls, sharp teeth, and eyes that **glowed** by the light of the **full Moon**, it is easy to imagine how they were feared and how tales of werewolves may have arisen.

Around the world

Myths about werewolves are found from medieval times to the 1900s; from the Beast of Gevauden in France, to P'an Hu, the dog-headed man in Chinese myths, to Lycaon in ancient Greece, where Zeus turned Lycaon into a wolf because he had served human flesh to the gods.

The Beast of Gevauden, a wolf-like creature, terrorized villages in France in the 1700s.

Some werewolf myths say that a werewolf transforms from man to wolf at a crossroads during a full Moon.

Lobishomem

Portuguese myths of werewolves, called Lobishomem, travelled to Brazil and Argentina with explorers in the 16th century. It was a widespread belief that the seventh male child in an all-boy family was a werewolf and some parents were known to be so scared of this that they abandoned their seventh male child.

Some myths say werewolves could be distinguished from real wolves by the lack of a tail.

Science and myth
Natural disasters

Experts believe that many elements of the Thunderbird myth have their roots in real events and creatures. In almost all cultures, for example, there is a great flood like the one that threatened the Quillayute tribe. And when the bird and the whale fight, the shaking ground and uprooted trees that result strongly resemble an earthquake. Dropping the whale into the ocean and flapping his wings ferociously, the Thunderbird disturbs the water in the same way as a tidal wave or tsunami.

Ancient creatures

The origins of the creature itself are not so clear. They may lie in Aiornis, a giant prehistoric bird that lived on the west coast of North America. This creature, which would have been alive when the first humans arrived, probably fed on dead whales. There are also many similarities between Thunderbird and the Pterodactyl dinosaur species – flying reptiles with good eyesight, a wingspan of up to 12 m (40 ft), and a big appetite for meat.

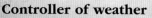

Controller of weather

For many native people, the Thunderbird figure is closely connected with one particularly complex part of nature – the weather. His eyes are thought to create sheet lightning, and lightning bolts are the glowing snakes he carries with him. Thunderbird creates storms since, not only do his wings stir the wind, but they also move rain clouds around the sky and make the sound of thunder, which is how the creature got its name.

Giant bird and monster whale

The folklore of many native North American tribes includes the powerful figure of a huge bird, usually called a **Thunderbird**. Each version of the myth is slightly different – sometimes he takes on human form and sometimes he's a spirit – either vengeful or protective.

Once, a long time ago, the Quillayute tribe was very hungry. For many days, there had been heavy rain and hail, so there was water everywhere, no crops were left in the ground, and hunters could find no whales or fish in the seas. Together, the people prayed to the Great Spirit for help. Then, after a long night of dark silence, there was suddenly a loud noise, flashes of lightning, and the low whirr of beating wings.

In the sky, a huge bird appeared – bigger by far than any they had ever seen. It had a curved beak with a sharp point at the end, and its eyes glowed brightly. When it came closer, they saw that it had a huge whale in its claws, which it dropped on the ground in front of them. The whale provided the Quillayute with everything they needed, and the Thunderbird

had saved them from hunger and death. But how had the Thunderbird caught the whale? In the story, there was always a great struggle – some say that when Thunderbird first captured the whale, he took it back to his mountain cave, and the whale fought so hard that the ground shook, and trees were torn up by their roots. Others claim that, during the battle, the whale escaped and returned to the water, but Thunderbird went after it again, flapping his huge wings and flashing his eyes. Thunderbird was always the winner.

For all the tribes that believe in him, Thunderbird is a figure of great power, wisdom, and magic, and his image is often reproduced as a symbol of respect. He has a hooked beak, sharp teeth, round, staring eyes, and big claws – sometimes he even wears a feathered crown, or headdress. He is often shown at the top of totem poles.

MAKE A TOTEM POLE

Use a kitchen roll tube for the pole. Glue on shaped pieces of card for Thunderbird's beak, ears, and wings, and for the whale's face and tail. Then decorate with pieces of sticky coloured paper.

Monsters of the deep

In centuries past, it was common for sailors to return from long
sea voyages with **terrifying stories** of huge sea creatures.
Some may have been figments of imagination,
but others may have simply been a
sailor's **first-ever** sighting of a real
sea creature such as a whale
or giant squid.

▶ **Kraken,** **Northern**
Europe Sailors lived in fear
of the Kraken, a huge sea
monster that could devour
ships and sailors. Sightings of
this fearsome creature may
well have been true, though
exaggerated, as giant squid
are known to grow to
12–15 m (40–50 ft).

▶ **Scylla, Ancient Greece** This sea monster lived in a cave near the island of Scilly opposite another sea creature called Charybdis, the source of whirlpools. Legend says that she was a beautiful sea nymph who was turned into a sea monster. She ate six of the companions of the hero Odysseus on their way home from the Trojan war *(see page 53)*.

◀ **Aspidochelone, Ireland**
Pliny the Elder, an ancient Greek historian, wrote about a large sea beast that enticed sailors onto its back in his book of Natural History. The Irish legend of Saint Brendan mentioned a similar creature. The sailors lit a fire on the "land" before they realized their mistake. The animal shuddered and the sailors ran in terror back to their ship.

▶ **Shachihoko,**
China and Japan
This sea monster has the head of a dragon and the body of a carp (a type of fish). Shachihoko statues were placed on roofs to protect the buildings from fire as it was believed the beast could make it rain.

◀ **Hydra, Ancient Greece** The Hydra was believed to guard the gates of the underworld that lay beneath the swampy lake in which it lived. It could regrow a head if one was cut off and according to legend, its breath could kill. It was eventually slain by Heracles *(see page 104)*.

Sacred animals of China

In **Chinese mythology**, animals often feature linked with people's **well-being**, **fate**, and **fortune**. These sacred animals had particular characteristics and are linked with superstitions, such as receiving wealth, luck, wisdom, and long life.

In Chinese myths, dragons are a positive symbol.

Chinese zodiac

Twelve animals are linked with the 12-year cycle of the Chinese calendar. People born in a particular year share the personality of that year's animal. According to legend, the order was decided by a race, with the rat coming first.

The Chinese unicorn is called the Kirin, or Chi-lin. It had the body of a horse and a head of a dragon with a single horn.

Supernatural animals

At the beginning of creation, the first god Pangu *(see page 12)* was helped by four sacred animals to create the world. These were the dragon, the phoenix, the tortoise, and the unicorn. When their work was finished they became the guardians of the hidden realms away from humans in the seas, the sky, the swamps, and the forests.

Spiritual guardians

According to myths, four creatures guard a different direction on a compass with the country of China in the centre. Each one is linked with a particular season, colour, element, and certain traits.

Red bird or phoenix
Summer, red, fire, and knowledge
Born out of fire, the phoenix guarded the south. The radiant bird was used as the symbol of the Empress of China.

Like a wild swan, it had a crane's forehead, a mandarin duck's crown, a swallow's throat , a chicken's beak, the back of a tortoise, and the tail from a fish with peacock's feathers.

Dragon
Spring, blue/green, wood, and abundance
Like a clawed snake, the dragon guarded the east. This powerful and fearsome creature was a symbol of the Emperor of China.

White tiger
Autumn, white, metal, and goodness
The powerful white tiger protected the west. The legends said the tiger would only appear during the peaceful reign of a virtuous Emperor.

The white tiger replaced the mythical Kirin.

S

E

W

N

With a snake's body, the dragon had deer's horns, a buffalo's head, nose and teeth of a lion, and claws from an eagle.

Black warrior
Winter, black, water, and happiness
The tortoise that guarded the north was often shown with a snake riding on its shell. Both these creatures are a symbol of long life.

Tortoise shells were burnt to judge good or bad luck in the future by the length of the crack formed.

The Monkey King

Birth
According to the myth, Monkey hatched from a stone egg created by the forces of chaos and the sky.

Equipped for success
Monkey learnt many skills as a student of a Taoist priest. He then tricked the Dragon King of the Eastern Seas into giving him a magical pillar that could grow and shrink to any size, cloud-walking boots, a phoenix-feather cap, and golden armour.

Heavenly court
In Taoist myths, the heavenly court had thousands of immortals that included heroes, scholars, emperors, priests and wise people as well as gods. The Jade Emperor ruled over this court.

Refined
The Jade Emperor attempted to execute Monkey for causing trouble by putting him into a sacred cauldron where the flames were hot enough to even burn up immortals. Because he was born of rock, Monkey not only escaped but became stronger and more powerful. Monkey now had the power to see evil in every form.

The Buddha challenged Monkey to jump into the palm of his hand. Thinking that would be easy, Monkey leapt. He landed in an empty space with just five pillars. He marked the central pillar and then leapt back, landing in Buddha's palm. Turning around, he saw that Buddha's middle finger was marked. Monkey had lost the bet.

Monkey King's mischief

In Chinese myths, one of the most loved characters is the mischievous Monkey King, **Su Wukong.** His escapades are told in a long novel known as **The Journey to the West.**

Monkey was clever – he could transform himself into 72 forms. He was agile – he could travel on clouds, leaping thousands of miles in a single somersault and was an unbeatable opponent in martial arts. He was cunning – he had tricked the Dragon King of the Eastern Seas into giving him magical possessions. But, above all, Monkey was ambitious – he had entered the underworld and crossed out his name from the book of judgement, so that he would never die and he believed that he should be the ruler of the heavens.

The Jade Emperor, who ruled the heavenly court of immortals, tried to control him but failed. In desperation, Buddha, the wisest of all, was asked to help.

Monkey lost the Buddha's challenge *(see left column)* and was imprisoned under a magic mountain to repent.

Five hundred years later, a gentle priest called Xuanzang was required to travel west to India to bring back the Buddhist scriptures to China. He would encounter many dangers on his journey so he needed protection. So, Monkey was asked to help.

Finally released after so long, Monkey willingly joined the humble priest and his two other companions: an exiled general, Sha Wujing, and a banished commander, Zhu Euneng (who had been transformed into a pig).

They travelled through imaginary lands where they were tested by many dangers.

On one adventure, they noticed the air getting hotter and hotter. The Fiery Mountains were ahead of them and the only way across was with a special plantain fan belonging to Princess Iron Fan.

However, the princess refused to give the fan to Monkey and instead, waved it and blew him away. But he returned with a wind-fixing pill in his mouth so that he could stand firm. This time the princess locked herself away, but Monkey turned into an insect, flew into the room, and landed in the tea she was drinking. She swallowed him and he caused her great pain. She agreed to give him the fan in return for leaving her alone, but she gave him a false one. So, Monkey returned for a third time, this time transformed into her husband, the Bull Demon King. However, once she gave him the fan, the actual Bull Demon King chased him and they fought fiercely. Pig and Sha Wujing joined in to help Monkey. With the plaintain fan, Monkey put out the demon's fire and escaped with his friends.

On their eventual return with the scriptures, they were all rewarded by becoming Buddhas and they flew up to live in the heavens.

MAKE A MONKEY KING MASK

Use a paper plate and snip two slits at the top and also at the bottom. Curve the plate to make a face shape, and staple or glue to fix the shape. Then cut out a nose and sticking-out ears.

Draw a monkey face onto the plate following the design opposite. (This design is inspired by the mask of the Monkey King used in Chinese opera.) Use paint or felt-tip pens to colour the design.

65

Crafty tricksters

Tricksters in myths, whether they are gods or goddesses, animals or spirits, men or women, all have one thing in common; they love having fun and making **mischief**. Often with no sense of what is right or wrong, they use **cunning** and deceit to get their way, though sometimes they end up looking rather foolish.

▲ **Eshu,** **West Africa** Eshu had an important job as messenger and mediator between the gods and the Yoruba people, but he loved creating mischief too. In one myth he even persuaded the Sun and Moon to change places.

▶ **Tengu,** **Japan** These trickster spirits are descended from Susano-O, the Shinto god of storms and the sea. Part bird part man, these demons play tricks on Buddhist monks and rob temples and those who do not respect them.

SEEING THINGS For more about Susano-O see page 103.

▲ **Kappa,** **Japan** Kappa were water spirits, famed for their wrestling skills, who liked to play tricks on people who went too close to their watery lair. Their strength came from water in a hollow on their head. If this water spilt, the kappa's power disappeared.

◄ Saci Perere, Brazil This one-legged prankster wears a magical red cap that gives him the power to appear and disappear. He is blamed for things going wrong, such as chickens not laying eggs or the cooking being burnt.

▲ Br'er Rabbit, North America The stories of Br'er Rabbit were invented for a children's book in the 1800s, but the tales were closely related to the hare and spider trickster tales brought over from Africa by slaves. Famous Br'er Rabbit stories also have links with native North American myths that tell of a trickster hare.

► Loki, Norse This mischievous god became more and more troublesome and nasty towards the gods of Asgard *(see page 90)*. He tricked the blind god, Hoder, into killing his gentle brother Balder with a piece of mistletoe.

► Krishna, India The Lord Krishna was famous even as a child for playing pranks. One tale tells of the god Brahma who wanted to test how clever Krishna was. He hid Krishna's cows to see if Krishna could find them again, but Krishna tricked him by creating identical copies of the cows and playing with them as if nothing had happened.

Anansi, the storyteller

The family tree

Anansi's father is Nyame, the sky god. His mother is Asase Ya, the Earth goddess.

The symbol for the sky god Nyame

Weaver and spinner of stories

Anansi stories began among the Akan people of Ghana, West Africa, then spread to tribes nearby and over the Atlantic Ocean with the slave trade. He is popular in the Caribbean, and in the south of America he is a "she", taking the name Aunt Nancy – truely an international traveller!

What's in a name

Anansi means "spider" in the Akan language. In the Americas, he is also called Nanzi, Ananse, Ananansa, and Annency.

Helper and friend

Ghanian myths say Anansi persuaded Nyame to create day and night, the Sun, Moon, and stars. He helped to bring rain to stop fires, and controlled how much the land flooded. He also taught people to make fire and how to grow food.

Many countries, many roles

Anansi is trickster or lovable rogue, a messenger and helper for Nyame, chief story keeper, and possessor of all wisdom.

Anansi, the wise spider

The sky god, Nyame, owned all the world's stories and there were none at all on Earth. Anansi wanted these stories, so he spun a web up to heaven to ask for them. Nyame set him **four tasks**. If he could capture Hornet, Python, Leopard, and Fairy and bring them to him, then he would give him the stories as a reward. Anansi was little, but fortunately what he lacked in strength he made up for with **brains**.

First he set about looking for Hornet, taking with him a gourd filled with water. Coming upon their nest, he threw some water over it and the rest over himself. The hornets came out, buzzing angrily. "Quick!" called Anansi. "Come and shelter from the rain inside my nice, dry gourd!"

Once the hornets had flown into the gourd, Anansi wove a thick web across the opening, trapping them inside.

Next he went to look for Python. He knew that he was very proud of how long he was, so he took a long branch and then went down to a stream muttering loudly all the while. "What are you mumbling about?" called Python from a tree nearby. "Well my wife thinks you are shorter than this branch, but I think you are longer," said Anansi. "I don't know how to convince her." "Well that's a simple matter to solve," said Python. "I'll lie along the branch and prove that I am longer." He stretched himself out along the branch and quick as a flash, Anansi bound him with a trailing vine so he could not move.

Now it was Leopard's turn. He dug a deep hole across the path that Leopard walked down every day and carefully covered it with branches and leaves. Then he sat down and waited patiently. Leopard came along later that day and fell right into Anansi's trap.

"Help! Someone help me!" he cried. "Here, grab my web. I'll pull you up," offered Anansi, coming out of his hiding place. As Leopard reached up, Anansi let down a sticky web of threads onto his head and bound him up tightly.

Finally, he set off to capture Fairy. He covered a doll in sticky gum and left it by a tree. Fairy came along and seeing the doll tried to pick it up. As soon as she touched the doll, she stuck fast and could not run away.

Anansi took the captives to Nyame who was delighted. He handed all of life's stories over to Anansi, and Anansi brought them down into the world to share with all people.

Eros **and Psyche**

Psyche (meaning "soul" or "spirit") was not a goddess – she was a mortal girl, one of three sisters, and by far the most beautiful. Some people thought she was even more beautiful than the ancient Greek goddess of love, **Aphrodite,** and this made Aphrodite very angry.

To punish her rival, Aphrodite sent her son Eros with his magic arrows. People who were pricked with these arrows fell in love with the first person they saw, and Aphrodite planned that Psyche would fall for a monster. Eros flew to Psyche's room while she was asleep. He drew one of his arrows, but she woke up and gazed at him. Startled by her beauty, he scratched himself with the arrow instead, and fell deeply in love with her. His mother was so enraged that she put a curse on Psyche, declaring that the girl would never marry. Eros turned to the god Apollo for help.

Not long after, Psyche's father, worried that she would accept no suitors, appealed to the oracle (fortune-teller) of Apollo to help her find a husband. He was told to leave her on a mountain top, where a powerful creature would take her for his wife. With great sadness, her parents followed the instructions. Soon, a soft wind carried Psyche to a beautiful place where she had everything she could want. At night, in the darkness, her husband came to her with warmth and gentleness and love, but she could not see his face, and he warned that she never would.

Soon, Psyche's sisters searched for Psyche, and found her. "What does he look like?" they asked. They were jealous, and they tormented her. "What if he's a beast who will devour you?" She was frightened, and that night, she took a lamp to bed so while her husband slept, she could make sure he wasn't a monster. She also took a knife, so if he were, she could kill him.

When all was dark and quiet, Psyche lit her lamp and shone it on her husband. What she saw made her gasp – of course, it was Eros, who had never stopped loving her. At that moment, a drop of lamp oil fell and woke him. When he saw what she'd done, he ran away, crying, "There can be no love where there is no trust".

Heartbroken, Psyche set out to find Eros and win him back.

Psyche opens the magic box.

All for love
The challenge
In desperation, Psyche turned to Aphrodite (see page 33), begging her forgiveness, and the goddess agreed to help if Psyche performed a series of impossible tasks. But Eros kept watch over Psyche, and made sure she could do everything Aphrodite asked.

The tasks vary slightly from one story to another, but almost all versions involved a magic box that Psyche had to bring back from the underworld, where it was guarded by the three-headed dog Cerberus. Psyche was warned never to open the box, but she couldn't resist. As soon as she lifted the lid, she fell into a deep sleep, but she was wakened by the ever-watchful Eros.

United at last
When Psyche completed all her "impossible" tasks, Aphrodite was even more furious than before, so Eros appealed to Zeus, father of the gods. Taking pity on him, Zeus fed Psyche on ambrosia, the food of the gods. This made her immortal, and therefore a suitable wife for Eros. In the end, Aphrodite set aside her jealousy, and accepted the union of Eros and Psyche.

Old story
Some historians believe that the tale of Psyche living in a beautiful palace with a mysterious creature is an older version of the 18th-century fairytale, *Beauty and the Beast*.

Plant legends

In myths, many plants are mentioned linked with **symbols** of life, healing, and death. But some stories provide **magical** explanations for the origin and appearance of certain plants.

▲ **Ceibo tree,** South America A young girl named Anahi, who loved to sing, was captured by an enemy tribe. She killed a soldier as she tried to escape but was caught again and burnt to death. As the flames, wrapped around her body she began to sing. Sunlight flooded into the camp and she was transformed into the ceibo tree with red flowers brightening the dense forest.

▶ **Coconut tree,** Guam
One day a beautiful girl became very thirsty. She asked for the juice from a special fruit. Everyone in her village tried to find the fruit, but was unable and the girl died. On her grave, a strange plant began growing. Five years later, it had reached 6 m (20 ft) tall and strange-looking fruits appeared. The fruit dropped and cracked open, revealing sweet liquid and chewy fruit, which the people called coconut.

▲ **Narcissus plant,**
Ancient Greece Narcissus was the name of a handsome but vain hunter, who fell in love with his own reflection in a pool. Unable to stop looking, he wasted away kneeling at the edge of the pool. According to the myth, the first Narcissus plant sprang up where he died, and is a symbol for vanity.

▲ **Dama de Noche,** Philippine
This is one of many tales of this scented night-time flower: Dama, a wife of a rich nobleman, asked the gods to give her a magic charm that would keep her husband by her side forever. That evening when he returned from yet another party, the nobleman could not find his wife, but instead could smell a glorious aroma. The amazing smell came from a new bush with thousands of tiny star-like white flowers outside his window. He never went out again but in the evening sat next to the bush, waiting for his wife to return. However, she was the bush.

SEEING THINGS
For more about
the god Apollo
see page 33.

▲ Palo Borracho tree, Argentina

Legend tells of a very beautiful girl who deeply
loved a warrior. When he went off to war, she
promised to love him always. A long time passed
and he never returned. In sadness, she went
into the forest to die. Hunters found her
but were unable to lift her as she was
rooted to the spot. Branches had begun
to grow from her body and white flowers
like tears bloomed from her fingers. The
flowers turned pink to remember the blood
shed by her warrior.

*Kokopelli was a native American spirit
of music and agriculture, shown as a
humpbacked flute player. Some myths say
the hump on his back is a sack containing
seeds of all the plants and flowers of the
world, which he scattered every spring.*

▲ Laurel tree, Ancient Greece

Eros, the mischievous god of love *(see page 71)*, sent a golden
arrow to Apollo, the Sun god, making him fall in love with
Daphne, a beautiful nymph. With a lead arrow, Eros made
Daphne hate Apollo. As Apollo chased Daphne, she cried out
to her father, the river god, to transform her shape. She was
changed into a laurel tree. Apollo continued to
love her and is shown wearing a crown of
Laurel. Lotis, another nymph Apollo chased,
became the lotus tree.

73

Midas, King of fools

Kind peasants take care of sleeping Silenus.

Long ago in Phrygia (which is now part of Turkey) there was a king called Midas, who was a good, but a very **foolish**, man. One day, local peasants came across an old satyr (a roguish woodland spirit, half man, half goat) sleeping in the countryside, and they carried him to Midas. The **satyr**, called Silenus, was drunk, and the peasants had tied him up with flower chains to stop him from wandering off.

Midas was a faithful follower of Dionysus, the god of wine and feasting, and he knew that Silenus was one of the god's closest companions. For several days, Midas looked after the satyr, fed him, made him comfortable, and kept him entertained. Eventually the king returned him to Dionysus, who lived on the banks of the River Pactolus. The god was so relieved to have his friend back safely that he offered to grant Midas any wish he chose. Midas asked that everything he touched be turned to gold. "Are you sure?" asked the god.

"Yes!" answered the king.

The wish was granted, and Midas set off for home. On the way, he brushed the twig of an oak tree, and it turned to gold. He rushed around touching everything he could find – a stone, an apple, a clump of soil – and it all turned to bright, shiny gold. When he arrived at his palace, he became more and more excited – he touched the gates, the roses in his garden, and the lanterns by his throne, and he was surrounded by gold. Midas called for food and wine (Dionysus' gift to the world), but when it touched his lips, it too turned to gold and he couldn't swallow it.

Suddenly, he understood why the god had questioned his wish. Just then, his beloved daughter reached out to comfort him, but as soon as his fingers reached her, she became a golden statue.

Terrified and grief stricken, Midas pleaded with Dionysus to free him from his terrible gift, and the god took pity.

"Find the source of this river (the River Pactolus)," he said, "and when you bathe in its waters, your gift will be washed away."

When the king obeyed, the river waters ran with gold, and he was free. To this day, there are flecks of gold all along the river's bank.

Final mercy
In some versions of the myth, Dionysus *(see page 33)* tells Midas to take the terrible golden statue of his daughter and bathe it in the river too. As soon as he does this, she returns to her human form.

More foolishness
The contest
Humbled by his own greed, Midas went to live in the countryside. Instead of following Dionysus, he began to worship Pan, the mischievous god of the fields, and master of music on reed pipes.

One day, Pan boasted that his playing was sweeter than the sound of Apollo's lyre (Apollo was the god of music and the Sun), and he challenged Apollo to a contest. Tmolus, the mountain god, was chosen to be the judge.

Pan played first, and everyone loved his merry tunes. But when Tmolus heard Apollo's haunting tones, he declared him the winner, and the people agreed – all except Midas. He not only disagreed – he declared the decision unfair.

The secret
Offended, Apollo turned Midas's ears into a donkey's long, furry ears. The king hid them under a turban and only his barber knew the truth. But the barber found it hard to keep the secret so he whispered it into a hole, which he then covered over. On that spot, a bed of reeds sprang up, and forever whispers in the wind, "King Midas has donkey's ears".

75

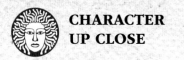
Biography
Nisse

What's in a name?
These little men were called Nisse "good lad" by the Norwegians and Danish. The Swedish called them "Tomtgubbe", "Tomte", or "Old Man of the House". "Tomte" refered to the ground under the house and the surrounding yard. Other names included "Gord-borde", "Gordvord", or "Tunvord", which mean protector.

Part of the family
Nisse were similar in character to the Brownie in Scotland, the Kobold in Germany, and the Kaboutermanneken of the Netherlands.

Home from home
Nisse liked to make their home somewhere where they can live undisturbed, such as a hayloft or attic, even under the floorboards. Some myths say that the Nisse was the soul of the farm's first inhabitant and lived in a burial mound.

A Nisse's reward
The family would give them small gifts to keep their good will, such as a little of the food they had prepared that day.

What, no butter!
One myth tells of a Nisse who flew into a rage and killed one of the cows because he didn't have butter on his porridge. However when he returned to finish his porridge he found the butter had just sunk to the bottom. Feeling remorseful, he went back and left money beside the dead cow to show he was sorry for his mistake.

Helpful **Nisse**

Every **Scandinavian farm** and household was once thought to have a Nisse. This **child-sized** old man was very helpful, but quick to get angry and cause trouble if people laughed at him, didn't appreciate him, or mistreated animals.

Be thankful or else...

If a farmer was thankful to the Nisse for even the smallest job, the success of his farm was guaranteed. However if he scorned the Nisse's help, he risked having tricks played on him, and the possibility of losing his "little helper" altogether.

Nisse tricks included spilling corn, tying cow's tails together, letting livestock loose, blowing out candles, and breaking things.

A Christmas connection

A novel written in the 1800s linked Nisse with the giving of gifts at Christmas (known as Jul). This idea grew in popularity and gave rise to the term Jultomten. These Nisse visited homes every Jul to check it was being cared for properly, giving presents to children who have been good.

According to legend, no farm did well unless it had a Nisse to help look after it. Often servants would wake in the morning to find the chores done and the barns swept.

Nisse loved to look after the livestock, but had a soft spot for horses. It was said that the farmer may look after the horse, but the Nisse kept it fat and healthy.

A bowl of porridge topped with honey or butter was a Nisse's favourite "thank you" gift.

Nisse were shy and disliked noise. They liked to keep out of sight when people were around.

Hidden folk

Mysterious little people who shy from human company and appear only at dusk are common in European mythology. They could be playful or mischievous, helpful or **vengeful,** and people were always careful in their dealings with them.

▼ **Elves,** **Northern Europe** The ancient stories of mischievous, harmful pointy-eared creatures called elves in England and Germany possibly had their origins in the Norse elf and dwarf myths. It was said that elves were responsible for bad dreams and illness. Back in the 10th century, a sudden pain in the side was widely thought to be caused by elves throwing things at you.

SEEING THINGS
For more about Norse myths see page 90.

▲ **Les Korrigans,** **France** These dwarf-like beings disliked the light, which showed them in their true, hideous form. They lived by springs near ancient stones and appeared dancing in circles at dusk.

▲ **Dwarfs,** **Northern Europe** The dwarfs in ancient myths were small, ugly, deformed creatures that lived in caves underground and were excellent metalworkers. They had very similar characteristics to the Norse dwarfs, Dvergar.

◀ **Leprechaun, Ireland** Famed for their shoemaking and hoarding crocks of gold at the end of the rainbow, some legends say that leprechauns are descended from the Tuatha Dé Danann – a group of Irish settlers in 1800s BCE, who lived in earth mounds.

▲ **Kobold, Germany** Usually invisible, these small, mischievous household spirits date back to ancient times. They could appear as animals, fire, people, or objects and had a reputation for helping or hindering people, depending on the way that they were treated.

▶ **Light elves, Norse** Two kinds of elves feature in Norse mythology. Light elves had magical powers and lived in Alfheim, a world between heaven and Earth, whereas the dark elves lived underground like dwarfs, and were greedy and unruly.

◀ **Huldufolk, Iceland** These hidden people are found throughout Scandinavian mythology. They were usually mild-mannered, however, terrible things apparently happened to those who deliberately damaged the large boulders in which they lived.

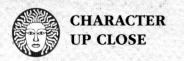
Biography
Bunyip

Creature of the swamp
There are many different descriptions of Bunyip, varying in shape, size, and colour. Some describe a half-human, half-animal creature, others describe the Bunyip as fish-like or gorilla-like.

Artists' impressions
In 1994, a set of four postage stamps was designed featuring images of the Bunyip. Was it like a medieval gargoyle (see above) or a part human part spirit guarding the waterholes (see below)?

This Bunyip had a flat tail for striking the water to lure people passing by into the murky depths.

Beware of **Bunyip**

In the deep waterholes and swamps in Australia, Bunyip lurks. This **evil** mythical spirit lures people into the black water and devours any person or creature it meets. Legends developed from stories of sightings and hearing loud **blood-curdling** cries.

Banished spirit...

Australian aborigines included this fearsome creature in their Dreaming stories. According to one myth, he was a tribesman who disobeyed the rules about how living things should live, which were set by the rainbow snake *(see page 20)*. Biami, the good spirit, punished the tribesman by banishing him from the tribe and telling all tribes to avoid him. In anger, the man became an evil spirit and was called Bunyip. He roamed the Earth at night, bringing unhappiness and fear to all the tribes, and devouring people, especially women and children.

... Or prehistoric hippo?

Up to about 40,000 years ago, a plant-eating marsupial about the size of a rhino lived in Australia. Known as a Diprotodon, it lived near water, grazing on shrubs and grasses. People have wondered if in fact these creatures survived and evolved into a hippo-like marsupial, which the early tribespeople saw and feared.

Diprotodon was the largest marsupial that ever lived. It was hairy and had sharp claws to dig up roots to eat.

Evil power

Aboriginal tales warn of terrifying fates if people came too close to Bunyip. Young women trapped by his power became water spirits, luring men into the water to drown.

Dark fur

Dog-like face

Goondah, a man fishing for eels, caught Bunyip's cub and in revenge was changed into a swan.

Walrus-like tusks or horns

A man and his wife from the Frog tribe separated by the Bunyip became trees whose branches leaned towards each other.

Strangers in the swamp
Since the 1800s, settlers claimed to have sighted Bunyips in marshes, lakes, and rivers in Australia and Tasmania. But were these "creatures" just people who had escaped from the law and hid away in swamps when someone approached? Thinking they were gone, they would emerge covered in mud and weeds and scream when they saw the intruder was still there.

Koala markings

So the legend goes, the marks on the face of a koala are a reminder to them to never talk to a Bunyip. Once a friendly Koala, every night, left her baby alone and went to chat to Bunyip by the waterhole. The other koalas, fearing that people would stop liking them, planned to stop her. An old koala put clay markings on his face and spoke to the spirits for magic. When Koala appeared he handed her baby to her and told the baby to never let go. The magic was strong and the baby held tightly. The Bunyip returned to the swamp tired of waiting.

Baba Yaga and Vasilisa the fair

The red horseman represents the noon-day Sun.

Baba Yaga, the witch
Old bony legs
The Russian witch, Baba Yaga was old, ugly, and impatient. However it was said that she kept her word once it was given. She flew through the air perched inside a mortar (a bowl for grinding), using the pestle to guide her. She used a broom to brush away her tracks. She had a huge appetite and ate children if they didn't complete her tasks.

The three horsemen
Baba Yaga, also known as "keeper of the light", controlled the Sun with the aid of three servants; one, dressed in white with a white horse, brought the dawn. A red horse and rider made the Sun rise into the sky. The last horseman was clad in black with a black horse; he represented night.

Vasilisa, the fair
Vasilisa's doll
Vasilisa's doll could have been a matrouska doll, a traditional wooden Russian doll with other dolls stacked inside it.

A happy ending
Vasilisa was cared for by an old woman after her stepmother died. With the doll's help she wove a cloth so beautifully soft and white that the old woman gave it as a gift to the Tzar (king). The Tzar, amazed by the quality of the cloth, asked for Vasilisa's hand in marriage.

Once there was a beautiful girl called Vasilisa, whose mother was very ill. Just before she died, she gave Vasilisa a **wooden doll** telling her it would look after her whenever she gave it food and drink.

Vasilisa's father remarried. His new wife and her two daughters hated Vasilisa because she was so beautiful. One day her father went away on business and her stepmother forced Vasilisa to do all the housework. Vasilisa was sad at being treated so badly, but was grateful for her doll, which helped her in her work.

One evening, the stepmother, her daughters, and Vasilisa were sewing when the fire burnt down and the candle went out. The stepmother ordered Vasilisa to fetch light from Baba Yaga, a witch who lived in the forest. Vasilisa was scared and very nervous, but was comforted that she had her doll.

While walking through the dark forest, Vasilisa was startled first by a white horseman and then by a red horseman. After a long, tiring day of walking another rider galloped by, this time dressed in black. He entered a clearing ahead and then disappeared.

In the clearing stood a strange-looking hut. It was made of bones and whirled about on chickens' legs. As Vasilisa stared, an ugly old witch appeared. It was Baba Yaga! Vasilisa nervously asked her for some light.

Baba Yaga croaked, "First you must work. If you do well, I will let you go; do badly, and I will eat you!"

The next day she made Vasilisa work all day, cleaning the hut. That evening she gave her some wheat and told her to pick out the mouldy grains. Vasilisa called on her doll for help, then fell asleep exhausted. When she awoke the next morning, the task was finished.

The second day Baba Yaga told Vasilisa to pick poppy seeds out from some dirt. Again the doll helped Vasilisa. When Baba Yaga asked how she had been so successful, Vasilisa told her that her mother's love had helped her. Knowing she could not compete with a mother's blessing, Baba Yaga gave Vasilisa a glowing skull and sent her home.

Vasilisa returned home and gave the light to her stepmother. To her surprise, the skull's eyes fixed on the stepmother and her two daughters. They burned so brightly and held their stare so tightly, that in the morning all that was left of Vasilisa's step-family were three piles of ash on the floor. Only Vasilisa was unharmed.

MAKE A BABA YAGA BIRD HOUSE

Use a square box for the hut, stiff card for the roof, and bendy wires or pipecleaners to twist into chicken legs for the feet.

Now add finishing touches such as a chimney made from modelling clay studded with gravel, moss on the roof, and drawings of bones on the walls.

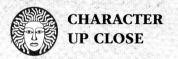
Biography
Sack Man

Creature of imagination
The appearance of this sinister creature varies around the world from a skinny or hairy man, a ghost, a giant blue blob that freezes the ground underneath its feet, or a green fog scratching at the windows. Some descriptions are connected with plants.

Persimmon
In Korea, the word for a persimmon, kotgahm, is also the name of the man with a sack. So the legend goes, a mother telling her crying child that she would feed him to a tiger if he did not behave was overheard by a passing tiger. The tiger waited for his meal, but instead the mother gave the child a persimmon to stop him crying. The tiger thought the persimmon must be a fiercer creature than he was.

Coconut head
In a child's imagination, a coconut as a head with three holes for the features of a face has become El Cuco (Coconut man). This is the name of the hairy little man in Spanish-speaking countries, such as Peru, Mexico, and Argentina.

Pumpkin face
In Portugal, El Cuco is a ghost with a pumpkin head. Following a tradition, hollowed out pumpkins with carved out eyes, nose, and a mouth, and a lit candle inside, are left in dark places to scare people.

Sinister *Sack man*

Lurking in the darkness, a **scary** "man" comes out, often at night, with a sack to snatch children who have not behaved. The children are never seen again… or so say parents all over the world to frighten their **misbehaving** children. Each country has a different name for him, such as Sack man or **Bogeyman.**

Truth in the tale

In Spain during the 16th and 17th centuries there were orphan collectors who collected abandoned babies. The babies were placed in a huge bag or a wicker basket. The collectors would carry on collecting more children all over the area before reaching the orphanage. Most of them died from lack of care in the bag. This is the likely origin of the myth about an ugly, skinny old man with a sack who snatches and eats misbehaving children.

An engraving of the Sack man by a Spanish artist

In Akita, people dress up as the Namahage demon and reenact the march around the village, going door-to-door to threaten to drag away disobedient children.

Here comes the Bogeyman!

Children who don't go to bed or don't sleep, children who suck their thumbs, and children who don't do as they are told - all (so parents say) may be taken away by the Bogeyman, who hides under beds or in wardrobes, waiting for night-time. In Japan, the Namahage is said to visit each house on New Year's Day and asks the parents if any lazy children or children who don't cry live there.

Quests and battles

Every culture has its legendary heroes – brave warriors who overcame great obstacles often with the help of the gods to achieve their heroic deeds. What qualities made them special and above the rest?

Perseus saves Andromeda from the fearsome sea creature by using the head of Medusa to turn it into stone (see page 110).

Warrior heroes

The **powerful** warrior hero is a popular character in legends and myths from every continent and many **epic** poems and sagas have been written about his adventures. These strong and **fearless** men will stop at nothing to fight for the causes they believe in.

◀ **Beserker, Norse** These were the most fierce of Viking warriors. They fought even when they were fatally wounded. It is from them that we get our word "berserk", meaning to be out-of-control with anger. Their battle frenzy was inspired by Odin, the god of war.

▲ **Cadmus, Phoenicia** Legendary founder of the ancient Greek city of Thebes and a mighty hero, Cadmus was famed for slaying a dragon that killed his companions. The goddess Athena ordered him to sow the dragon teeth in the ground, where they sprouted and grew into a fierce race of warriors called the Spartoi.

▲ **Achilles, Ancient Greece** When Achilles was born, his mother dipped him in the river Styx to make him invincible. However the heel she held him by remained unprotected. As an adult his exploits as a warrior were legendary, but he was finally killed by an arrow to his heel!

SEEING THINGS
For more on Achilles see page 112.

▲ **King Arthur and his knights,** England An ancient legend says that King Arthur and his knights of the Round Table sleep in a hidden cavern, ready to rise and fight to save Britain if they are ever needed *(see pages 122)*.

▲ **Hildebrand,** Germany In the poem *Hildesbrandlied*, a warrior, Hildebrand, leaves his son when young, but meets him years later as they stand on opposing sides in battle. Hildebrand recognizes his son, and offering him his arm rings, suggests they lay down their weapons. His son refuses, suspecting an enemy trick. Hildebrand knows he will have to fight and kill his son, or be killed.

▲ **Yamato Takero,** Japan
This legendary hero possessed a terrible temper. Sent into exile for killing his brother, his strength and quick wits, together with a sacred sword from the god Susano-O, helped him evade his enemies.

▶ **Arjuna,** India
Arjuna, seen here with Krishna, was called "Jishnu", the undefeatable. He was a skilled archer with a strong sense of duty.

▲ **Fionn Maccumhail (Finn MacCool),** Ireland Hero of the Irish people, Fionn formed a band of fighters into an elite fighting force in order to protect Ireland against invaders.

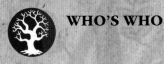

Norse gods

The Vikings were ruthless warriors, raiding countries far and wide from their native Norway, Sweden, and Denmark. Their gods and the mythical realms reflected the **fearless warrior instinct** of the people and the harshness of their land. The Vikings believed their gods would honour them for **bravery**.

Yggdrasil
Vikings believed a great ash tree towered over the world and its roots and branches supported the nine realms of the world.

Jotunheim
Land of the giants

Vanaheim
Land of the Vanir, the older fertility gods, including Njord, Freyja, Freyr, Idun, and Siff

Szartalfheim or Nidavellir
Land of the dark elves (dwarfs)

Asgard
Land of the Aesir, the war gods

Alfheim
Land of the good elves

Midgard
Land of people

Muspellheim
Land of heat and fire; this was the second world created.

Helheim
Land of the dead

Niflheim
Land of darkness and ice; this was the first world created.

Animals of Yggdrasil

The eagle Hraesvelg sat on the topmost branch of the ash tree, causing the wind by flapping his wings. Four stags kept the tree pruned, and a dragon Nidhogg gnawed at its roots and quarrelled with the eagle. A squirrel named Ratatosk scurried up and down the tree's trunk delivering spiteful messages between the dragon and eagle.

Odin
Ruler of the gods, god of magic, poetry and prophecy, battle and death
He is recognized by his long flowing robes and large beard. He has one eye that shines as brightly as the Sun. He traded his other eye for wisdom.

ODIN AND FRIGG
MARRIED. THEY HAD MANY SONS.

Frigg
Goddess of marriage and motherhood
She knew the destiny of everyone but never revealed what she knew.

Vidar
A strong, silent, and vengeful god
He avenged his father's death by killing the wolf Fenrir at Ragnarok, the last battle.

Thor
Ruler of the skies, storms, and thunder
(see page 92)
He can be recognized by his red hair. He wears iron gloves and a magic belt, and wields a hammer.

Days of the week
Four of the English names for the days of the week have come from the names of the Norse gods: Tyr in Tuesday, Thor in Thursday, Frigg in Friday, and Odin (who was known as Woden) in Wednesday.

Balder
A wise and beautiful god so the light shone from him
Loved by other gods, he was protected from harm, except from mistletoe, which killed him.

MARRIED
Nanna
An Asyniur, a powerful goddess
After Balder's death, she died of grief and they were both united again in Helheim.

Hoder
A blind, very strong god
He was fooled by the trickster god Loki, into killing his brother Balder.

Njord
God of wind and sea

MARRIED
Skadi
Goddess of skiing and hunting
They were not happy.

Skadi

Hermod
Messenger god
He was bold and brave, and volunteered to enter Helheim to beg for the release of Balder.

Freyr

Bragi
God of poetry and eloquence
He entertained the gods and greeted the dead heroes in the meeting hall of Valhalla.

MARRIED
Idun
Goddess of eternal youth
She guarded the golden apples that were eaten by the gods to stop them growing old and dying. The trickster, Loki, caused her to be taken by a giant, but was forced to rescue her.

Tyr
God of war
When the gods bound the wolf Fenrir with a magical silken cord, Tyr placed his hand in its mouth as a pledge, and the wolf bit it off.

Heimdall
Guardian of the gods
Born of nine sisters, he watched over the rainbow bridge, Bifrost, which linked Asgard, the land of the gods, to Migard, the land of humans. He's shown holding a horn, which he used to alert the gods of intruders.

Idun sharing her golden apples.

Forseti
God of justice and reconciliation
He ruled from the glittering court of justice named Glitnir in Asgard.

Freyja
Goddess of love, beauty, and magic
She was also a goddess of war. She received half of the warriors who fell in battle, while Odin received the other half.

Freyr
God of peace, weather, and prosperity
He was twin brother to Freyja. He died at the last battle of Ragnarok because he lent his magic sword, which could fight on its own, to his servant Skirnir.

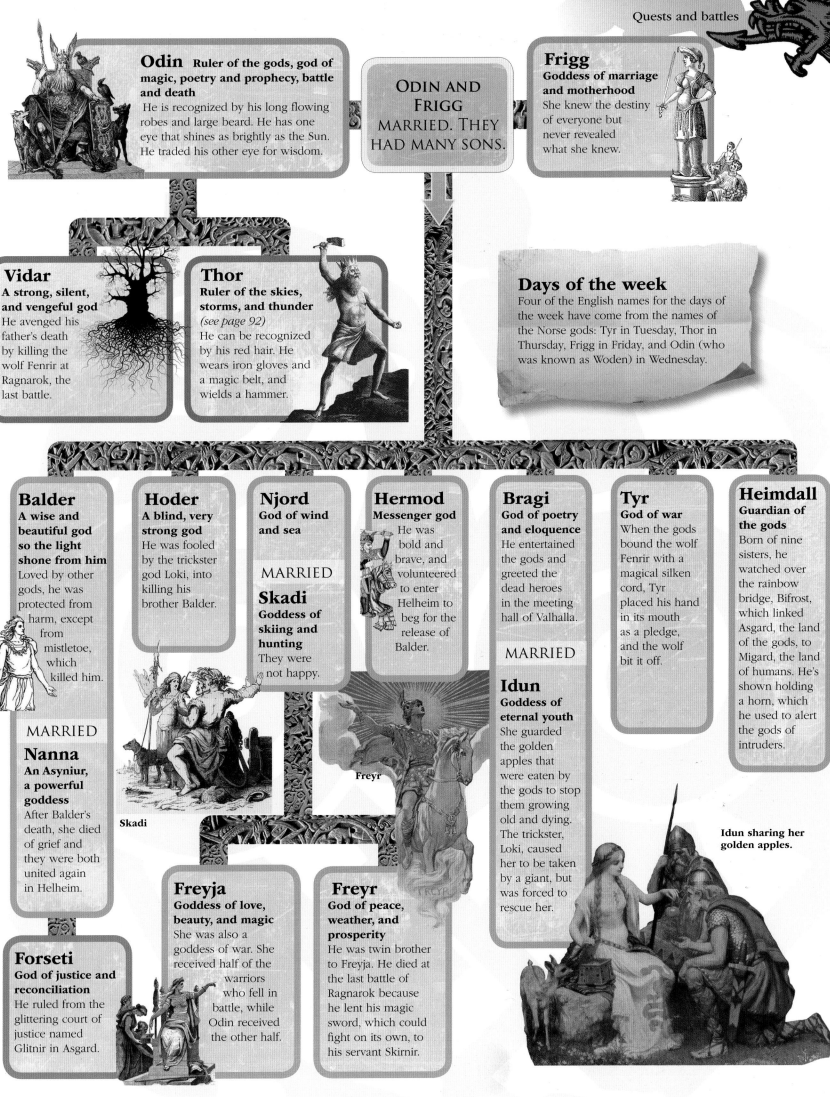

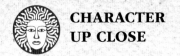

CHARACTER UP CLOSE

Biography

Thor, god of thunder and weather, and fertility

Family connections

Thor was the son of Odin, ruler of the gods, and the giantess Jord, (Earth).

Odin, father of Thor

He was married to Siff, who was famous for her long gold hair. When the trickster god Loki cut this off, the dwarfs forged new hair of real gold for her.

Siff's golden hair was cut by the mischievous god, Loki.

Thor also had a mistress the giantess Jarnsaxa and had two sons, Magni and Modi, meaning "Strength" and "Fury".

Thor's realm

In Asgard, the realm of the gods, Thor lived in Thrudvangr (Power-field) or Thrudheimr (Power-home). There stood his golden-roofed Hall, Bilskirnir.

Iron gloves,
Jarngreipr

Hammer,
Mjollnir

Magic belt,
Megingjord

Thundering **Thor**

One of the most popular gods of the **Vikings** was Thor, the hot-tempered, red-headed, hammer-wielding god of the skies. There are many myths of his frequent battles against the gods' main enemies, **the giants**, but his greatest foe was the Midgard serpent *Jormungandr*, which was so huge it encircled the world beneath the sea.

Thunderstorms

Thor was well known for quickly losing his temper. Thunder would roll as he rode through the heavens on his chariot drawn by two goats called Tanngnjostr (Teeth Grinder) and Tanngrisnir (The Snarler). Lightning flashed as he wielded his magic hammer – with extra strength provided from his magic belt – onto the heads of the giants.

Tanngnjostr and Tanngrisnir

Ragnarok, the last battle

Thor's fiercest battle was foretold to come at the end of the world, when he would fight and kill his arch-enemy, the serpent Jormungandr at the battle of Ragnarok. Thor himself would be killed by the serpent's poisonous breath. Ragnarok is sometimes translated "Twilight of the gods", for almost all of them are destined to die.

On one attempt, Thor caught the serpent with the bait of an ox's head, but the giant Hymir was so frightened he cut the line before Thor could bring his hammer down.

Thor's magical hammer, Mjollnir, was crafted by the dwarfs Brok and Eitri as part of a bet with the trickster god, Loki. Loki gave the hammer to Thor to prevent him taking revenge for cutting his wife's hair.

Going for gold

On the river bed, the golden hoard is guarded by three water nymphs called Rhinemaidens.

Ancient and modern
Epic poem
This legend is one of many that originated as epic (story) poems. The first (known) mention is in the 10th-century Latin work Waltharius. We know from rune-marked stones found in Scandinavia (runes are early picture letters) that it's part of Norse (early Scandinavian) mythology, and it's also told in the German epic Nibelungenlied (Song of the Nibelungen). This dates from the Middle Ages, when epic poems were a popular form of story telling.

Successful opera
In the modern world, the story of the Nibelungen is most familiar in the form of Richard Wagner's Ring cycle (series) of four operas – The Rhinegold, The Valkyrie, Siegfried, and Twilight of the Gods. In Wagner's retelling, the Nibelungen are a race of dwarfs, and many of the other characters are gods, ruled by their king, Wotan.

The ring
Alberich, a dwarf, steals a hoard of magic gold from the Rhine, and forges it into a ring. Many of the gods are involved in a twisted plot to get the ring away from Alberich, and when they do, he puts a curse on it. In this tale, Wotan arranges for Siegfried, his grandson, to win the ring, but Siegfried is betrayed and killed. Eventually, Brunnhilde, Wotan's daughter, returns the ring to the Rhine, but in the process, all the gods are destroyed.

One of the best-known myths of northern Europe involves the **Nibelungen**, a wicked family who owned a **magic hoard of gold**. This legend appears in lots of different versions, many set in the **land of the ancient Burgundians.**

In the stories, the Nibelungen are their royal family, who lived near the River Rhine in what is now Germany. The saga's hero is Siegfried, a German warrior who killed two Nibelungen chiefs and captured their magic sword, their invisibility cape, and their magic gold. However, before they died, the chiefs put a powerful curse on their treasure.

Siegfried and Brunnhilde

94

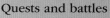

Fired up by his victory, Siegfried pursued the lovely Kriemheld, sister of the king, Gunther. Hagan, Gunther's evil brother, wanted the precious hoard for himself, so he warned Gunther against Siegfried, but Siegfried won Gunther's trust by fighting with him against his great enemies, the Saxons.

Gunther agreed to the marriage between Siegfried and Kriemheld, but only on condition that the warrior helped him win the hand of Brunnhilde, the beautiful Icelandic queen. Together, Gunther and Siegfried set out for Iceland, and, concealed under his magic cloak, Siegfried overpowered Brunnhilde. Later, believing that Gunther was the strong warrior who captured her, she agreed to marry him, and Siegfried married Kriemheld.

But Brunnhilde was horrified to discover that she was married to Gunther, not Siegfried, and her feelings made Gunther jealous. Under orders from his king, the willing Hagan murdered Siegfried. Kriemheld, assuming she'd inherited the magic hoard, vowed to use it to avenge her husband's death. But Hagan, after seizing the treasure he always wanted, threw it into the Rhine for safety, choosing a special place that was known only to him.

All in a name

This legend has many sources, so the names vary. In the Latin poem, the Nibelungen are Nivilones. In the Norse sagas, Siegfried is Sigurd – the common "Sig" means victory. And Etzel in the German poem is also known as Attila, King of the Huns, but this isn't the same Attila who troubled ancient Rome.

Years later, Kriemheld took her revenge – she married Etzel, king of the Huns, then lured Gunther and Hagan to Etzel's court and had them killed. Later, their followers killed her. The secret hiding place of the Nibelungen gold was buried with Hagan, so it still lies undiscovered at the bottom of the Rhine.

Mythical creatures

Mythical beasts are **extraordinary looking**. Often terrifying to behold, they are created from the body parts of different animals and possess **supernatural** powers. Many are evil, but some are helpers of the gods and a few (including the unicorn) represent goodness.

▼ Manticore, India There was much debate in ancient Greece as to whether this man-eater, with a red lion's body, a man's face, and a scorpion tail that fired poisonous thorns, could possibly exist.

▶ Garuda, India
In Hindu and Buddhist mythology, the eagle-headed god Garuda is revered as the mount of the god Vishnu and the destroyer of evil. Garuda is the sworn enemy of snakes (nagas) and people wear his image to protect them from snake attacks.

▼ Chimera, Ancient Greece A fire-breathing monster, the Chimera was a mix of lion, goat, and dragon. It lived in the mountains of Asia Minor, killing all it met, until killed by the hero Bellerophon. Riding on the winged horse, Pegasus, he used his spear to push a lump of lead into the Chimera's throat, where it melted in the heat and suffocated the creature.

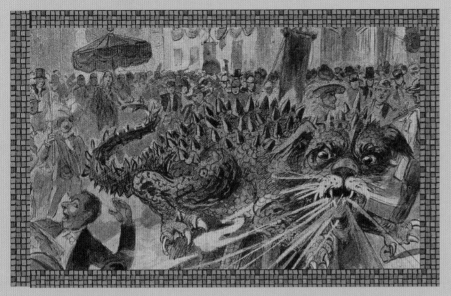

▲ **Tarasque, France** This fierce, turtle-backed beast was said to terrorize villages in southern France, burning all it touched. As the offspring of the Leviathan of the Bible and Onachus, a scaly beast from Spain, it was eventually tamed by Saint Martha.

▶ **Unicorn, France** The unicorn's horn was said to have magical, life-giving powers. Ground horn was sold as a medicine in medieval times, but it was probably powdered narwhal horn instead.

◀ **Centaur, Ancient Greece** The savagery of these wild forest creatures who were half man and half horse was well known. However one, Chiron, was famed for his wisdom and kindness.

▼ **Griffin (Gryphon), Europe, Asia** Known for their strength, these ferocious-looking lion eagles built nests out of gold and guarded them fiercely. Griffin myths may have arisen from the discovery of fossilized dinosaur bones.

◀ **Draugen, Norse** These monsters lived in the graves of Vikings and haunted the living. In modern folklore, draugen have been connected with drowned sailors. If seafarers saw a draugen rowing half a boat, they knew they were doomed.

Indian gods

The myths of India combine the gods of the early **Vedic** stories and the slightly later gods and goddesses of the Hindu stories. The stories show people how best to **lead their lives**. In the background of all the stories are the all-powerful three central **Hindu** gods, Lord Brahma, Lord Vishnu, and Lord Shiva.

Matsya, the fish *Kurma, the tortoise* *Varaha, the boar* *Narasingha, the lion* *Vamana, the dwarf* *Parasu-rama, the warrior* *Rama, the prince* *Krishna, the king* *Buddha, the spiritual leader* *Kalki, still to come*

Ten avatars
When the balance of good and evil in the universe became disrupted, Lord Vishnu took an earthly form to set it right. There have been nine avatars (forms) or incarnations of Vishnu. The tenth, Kalki, is his future incarnation, which he will become at the end of the world, Kali Yuga.

Lord Vishnu
Preserver and protector
Connected with peace, goodness, and mercy, he's responsible for the daily running of the universe. He holds a conch, a disc, a club, and a lotus.

BRAHMA, VISHNU, AND SHIVA ALL CAME FROM THE SAME SUPREME BEING NAMED BRAHMAN.

Saraswati
Goddess of knowledge
Dressed in white, she holds a mala (beads) and a palm-leaf scroll as symbols of knowledge. She plays the veena, an Indian stringed instrument.

Lord Brahma
Creator
He grew in a lotus out of the navel of Vishnu and made a goddess out of himself, Saraswati, to help him create the world.

Devas and demons
During creation, Lord Brahma formed many wise sages, who appear in the Indian myths. One of these, Kashyap fathered the demi-gods, who were the gods of natural forces, and their archenemies, the demons, who constantly fought them and caused disruption. The demons always lost the battles because Brahma, Vishnu, and Shiva supported the demi-gods.

Indra, the king of the demi-gods *Varuna, the god of the oceans* *Vayu, the god of wind* *Agni, the god of fire*

Ravana, the ten-headed demon king

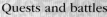

Calming the Ganga

The River Ganges is considered sacred because it is believed that the waters used to flow through the heavens. One day, Ganga, a pretty goddess, insulted a wise sage and his curse turned her into a river. In the story of Bhagiratha, an Indian king, Ganga was sent to flow down onto the Earth by Brahma. She didn't want to go but could not disobey him, so in anger she decided to flood the whole Earth in her powerful fall. However, as she roared down, Lord Shiva stepped in her way and trapped Ganga in his hair. He made her gently flow through his long hair onto the mountains of the Himalayas.

Lord Shiva controlling the flow of the River Goddess Ganga.

Lakshmi
Goddess of light, beauty, wealth, and good fortune
She is often shown on an opened lotus, meaning purity. The gold coins pouring from her hand symbolizes wealth.

Lord Shiva is also known as the Lord of the Dance because he controls creation through his wild dances.

Parvati, Lakshmi, and Saraswati, are all forms of the divine female power, Mahadevi. Other forms are Durga (see page 100) and Kali, the goddess of death and destruction.

Lord Shiva
Destroyer
He balances creation and destruction and can destroy the universe to remove imperfections so that it can be re-created. He has a third eye for wisdom.

Parvati
Goddess of courage and power
As the wife of Shiva, she keeps him calm through her love and patience, teaching him about happy family life.

Kartikeya
Leader of the devas' armed forces
As a perfect and brave son of Shiva, he was created to fight and destroy the demons and any evil.

Ganesha
God of success This popular elephant-headed god banishes all evils and removes all obstacles to help humans achieve success.

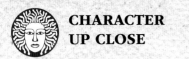

CHARACTER UP CLOSE

Biography
Durga, Mother of the universe

What's in a name?
Durga's name means "the inaccessible".

Multiple forms
She appears in many forms as aspects of the great goddess, Mahadevi, the divine female power that existed at the beginning of creation. Her forms include:

Parvati, the caring, gentle goddess of courage, Lakshmi, the goddess of light and wealth, Kali, the goddess of death and destruction, Saraswati, the goddess of wisdom, and Sati, the goddess of long life.

Kali   *Saraswati*

Family connections
In her gentle aspect of Parvati, she is wife of Shiva, the destroyer.

As Parvati, she has two sons Kartikeya, leader of the devas' armed forces, and Ganesha, god of success, and daughter Jyoti, goddess of light and knowledge.

Ganesha

100

Goddess **Durga**

The stories about the invincible Hindu **warrior goddess,** Durga, are tales of ferocious battles with demons. She has great destructive power, but uses this to **triumph over evil.** Her role is to keep order on Earth, in the heavens, and throughout the universe.

Lethal foe

All the gods combined their energies to create Durga, when Earth, heaven, and the universe were threatened by the buffalo demon, Mahishasura, and his army. She was born fully-grown. When fighting the demons, the other gods gave her their weapons to use:

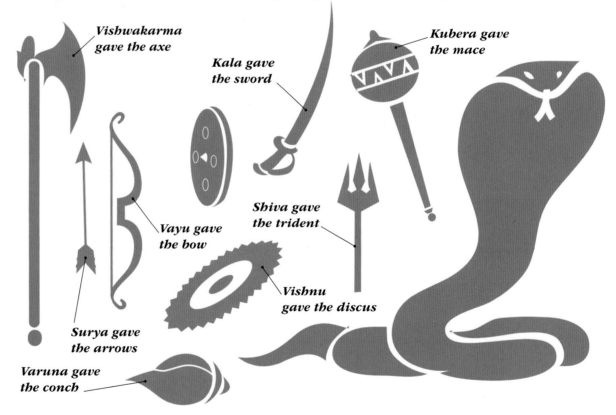

Vishwakarma gave the axe

Kubera gave the mace

Kala gave the sword

Vayu gave the bow

Shiva gave the trident

Surya gave the arrows

Vishnu gave the discus

Varuna gave the conch

Epic battle

During the battle, the demon Mahishasura changed his form into many different creatures, such as a buffalo, an elephant, and a lion, each time Durga slew him. Finally, Durga paralyzed the demon as he was changing shape by producing an amazing light from her body and then cutting off his head.

Durga is shown having eight or ten arms, representing the eight areas or ten directions of Hinduism. This symbolizes that Durga is protecting the worshippers from all directions.

Red clothes symbolizes action because she is always busy destroying evil and protecting from pain and suffering.

Durga has three eyes; the left eye represents desire, the right eye represents action, and the central eye represents knowledge.

One hand holds a lotus flower that isn't yet in full bloom. This means that success in battle is certain but not yet achieved.

The conch shell produces the sound of creation and victory over evil.

She rides a lion or a tiger to represent power, will, and determination.

Okuninushi and the white rabbit

The Izumo Cycle is a series of myths about the gods who lived in the Izumo area of **western Japan**. **Susano-O**, the storm god, was banished from the heavens because he was annoying his sister **Amaterasu**, the Sun goddess *(see page 18)*. He married the Princess of the Rice Paddies and together they settled in Izumo. Their son **Okuninushi** was an important character in the stories.

Okuninushi had 80 brothers and they all wanted to marry a beautiful princess called Ya-gami-hime. The brothers set off ahead, leaving Okuninushi to carry the baggage. On their way, they met a rabbit that was in great pain because it had lost all its fur.

"What can I do to grow back my fur?" pleaded the rabbit.

"Bathe in salty water," replied the wicked brothers and they went on their way. When the rabbit did this, it only made its pain worse.

A little while later, Okuninushi met the suffering rabbit. "How did you lose your fur?" asked Okuninushi kindly. The rabbit began to recount its sorry tale:

"I was on my way to visit Princess Ya-gami-hime and needed to cross the water between our islands. I said to a crocodile that my family had more members than his. It disagreed, so I suggested that

all his family line up from shore to shore and I would count them. They did as I asked, and I was able to hop across their backs. As I neared the shore, the crocodiles realized that I had tricked them, and the last one seized me and tore off my skin as I escaped. What can I do to grow it back?"

"Bathe in fresh water and then roll in the seeds of a cattail reed," suggested Okuninushi.

The rabbit followed his instructions and its fur grew back. The rabbit then revealed itself to be a god, and promised Okuninushi that he would marry the princess.

His brothers were very jealous and angry. They rolled a white-hot boulder down a mountain towards Okuninushi. Thinking it was a boar, he grabbed it and burnt to death. But the gods revived him. The brothers then crushed him to death, but again the gods brought him back to life and he fled to the underworld where his adventures continued.

Susano-O fights a water dragon.

The story continues...
Further trials
In the underworld, Okuninushi met his half sister, Suseri-hime, who he fell in love with. But their father Susano-O was not happy about this and wanted Okuninushi to prove himself a worthy husband and set him some difficult tasks. Suseri-hime helped him to succeed but their father still refused to let them marry.

The elopement
So one night, while Susano-O slept, Okuninushi crept into his room and tied his long hair to the rafters of the palace. Then taking his father's weapons and a musical instrument called a koto, he ran away with Suseri-hime. When Susano-O awoke he had to pull down the palace before he could give chase.

The ruler
Okuninushi and Suseri-hime left the underworld. He used his father's weapons to fight his brothers and then became a powerful ruler of Izumo. Later he became the god of abundance, medicine, magic, and happy marriages.

PERFORM A PUPPET SHOW
Make a rabbit finger puppet using felt and other material. Use an old sock or an old woollen glove for the crocodile. Glue on some googly eyes and strips of material for its teeth, tongue, and bumpy back. Now you're ready to retell the story using your puppets.

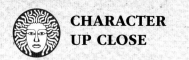
Biography
Heracles

Family connections
Also known as Hercules by the Romans, he was the son of Zeus (Roman name: Jupiter) and a human, Alcmene. Hera, Zeus's wife, was angry with Zeus but took her anger out on Heracles instead.

Heracles wrestles the Nemean lion with his bare hands.

The twelve labours of Heracles
1. Kill the Nemean lion.

2. Slaughter the Hydra. Heracles burnt off its eight mortal heads and buried the immortal one.

3. Capture the Cernean hind (stag) with gold antlers and brass hooves.

4. Bring back the Erymanthian boar alive.

5. Clean 30 years of filth from the Augean stables in a day.

6. Kill the Stymphalen birds, which ate human flesh.

7. Capture the crazed Cretan bull.

8. Tame the flesh-eating mares of King Diomedes.

9. Steal Hippolyta's belt (she was Queen of the Amazons).

10. Capture Geryon's cattle.

11. Fetch the golden apples of the Hesperides.

12. Bring the three-headed dog Cerberus from Tartarus.

Heracles, the hero

The **mighty** Greek demi-god and hero Heracles was often persecuted by Hera, Zeus's wife. On one occasion she made him fly into a rage and kill his family. Full of remorse, he sought advice at the Delphi Oracle. His **penance** was to complete a set of "impossible" tasks set by King Eurystheus. Only then could he achieve immortality and forgiveness.

Poisoned blood

Heracles had further exploits after his twelve tasks. While crossing a river, Nessus the centaur tried to abduct Heracles' new wife Deianeira. Heracles killed him with an arrow poisoned with the Hydra's blood. But before Nessus died, he convinced Deianeira to keep some of his blood saying it is a love potion that cured unfaithfulness.

Nessus knew his blood was now deadly poison and would kill Heracles if ever used on him.

Heracles' death

Heracles pleads to Zeus who takes pity on him and gives him immortality, rescuing him from death.

Years later, Deianeira heard rumours that Heracles was being unfaithful. Unaware that Nessus had tricked her, she spilt some of Nessus's blood onto Heracles robe. Heracles put the robe on and immediately writhed in agony as the poison burned him. Heracles persuaded a friend to burn him on a funeral pyre to free him from his pain.

Heracles wore a lion's skin, using its head as his helmet. He killed the lion when it attacked his father's cattle.

Heracles always carried a wooden club as a weapon.

Heracles' father was a god, so he was partly immortal. This meant he was stronger, bigger, and more skillful than any man.

Even as a child, Heracles was incredibly strong, strangling two snakes with his bare hands.

Heracles' sister Athena
Athena was Heracles' half sister, daughter of Zeus and goddess of war. She helped him achieve three of his quests; she gave him clappers to scare the Stymphalen birds, returned the apples of Hesperides for him, and led Cerberus out of the underworld.

Heracles and Hermes worship at Athena's altar, seeking her protection.

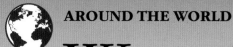
Warrior heroines

Heroines appear in myths and legends as **protectors**, saviours, fighters, or they disguise themselves to play the traditional male role of **warrior**.

▼ **Joan of Arc,** France Joan was said to have been just 13 years old when she was told in a vision of St Michael to join the fight against the English. It was said that the saints led her to find her sword buried behind a church altar. Although old and rusty, the rust magically fell away when she picked it up.

SEEING THINGS
For more about the Trojan Wars see pages 112.

▲ **Amazons,** Ancient Greece This nation of warrior women was led by a queen, Hippolyta, who was said to be the daughter of the Greek god of war, Ares. They had a reputation for being strong, cunning fighters. The epic poem the *Iliad* by Homer says that the Amazons fought for Troy after the Trojan warrior Hector was killed.

▲ **Buffalo-Calf-Road-Woman,** North America The Cheyenne nation renamed a battle with Custer's men in Buffalo-Calf's honour after she galloped into the thick of the fighting at Rosebud Creek to save her brother. Her courage persuaded the others to continue fighting.

▼ **Oya, West Africa** Goddess of the Niger River, Oya is also known as warrior goddess of the wind, lightning, and destruction by the Yoruba people. As she dances, her whirling skirts create tornadoes.

▲ **Hua Mu lan, China** This heroic warrior disguised herself as a man and joined the army to save her aged father from having to fight. She excelled as a leader, but after the fighting chose to go home to her family rather than remain in the army.

◀ **Boudicca, England** Queen of the Iceni tribe, Boudicca led an uprising against the Romans early in their occupation of England. Legend has it that she fought hard and long, but was eventually defeated, although the location of her defeat and burial remain unknown.

▶ **Bellona, Ancient Rome** Some myths say she was the twin sister to Ares, the god of war. Romans would pray to her to ask that she would give them a war-like spirit when fighting.

Historically, a labyrinth was a maze with just one path to the centre. But in mythology, a labyrinth is a test the hero must overcome – a symbolic life journey from birth (the start) to death (the middle).

Theseus the hero
Parents
Theseus's mother was Aethra, daughter of King Pittheus. He had two fathers: Aegeus, Aethra's husband and the king of Athens, and Poseidon, the sea god.

Claim to the throne
After Aegeus discovered that Aethra was pregnant, he returned to Athens. He left behind his sword and sandals, burying them under a heavy rock. He told Aethra that if their son was a hero he would lift the rock, find the tokens, and come to claim the throne of Athens.

Theseus's journey to Athens
When he grew up, Theseus found the sword and sandals, and set out for Athens. He faced six challenges on the way, each one a threat to his life, but he overcame them all.

Attempt on Theseus's life
Theseus's stepmother wanted her own son to inherit the kingdom, so tried to kill Theseus. He survived one challenge and, at the second attempt, was saved from drinking poison by his father Aegeus.

Heroic quests
Theseus appears in many Greek legends. One tells of his rescue of princess Hippodamia from centaurs.

Theseus and the Minotaur

King Minos of Crete, son of Zeus (king of the gods), boasted that the gods favoured him. He asked the sea god Poseidon for a **white bull** to sacrifice to them. However, Poseidon sent such a fine white bull that Minos refused to use it as a sacrifice. As **punishment,** the goddess of love Aphrodite made Minos's wife Pasiphae fall in love with the bull. They had a son, the **Minotaur,** that was half man half bull, and hid it in a labyrinth.

The kingdoms of Crete and Athens were old enemies, ever since King Aegeus of Athens had accidentally helped to kill King Minos's son. In return, King Minos demanded that, every nine years, Aegeus must send him seven boys and seven girls. The children were put into the labyrinth as food for the Minotaur.

The third time this was due to happen, Aegeus's son Theseus offered to be sent so he could kill the Minotaur. The king was reluctant to let him go, but knew that Theseus was strong and there was a chance he could succeed.

He told his son, "The boat the children sail in has black sails as a sign of mourning. I will also send you with black sails – but as a sign of hope, there are white sails too. If you return, raise the white sails so we know you have been successful."

When Theseus arrived in Crete, he told King Minos that he was the son of Poseidon and had come to kill the Minotaur. "If I am successful, Athens will no longer be in your debt."

King Minos mocked him, so Theseus dived to the ocean-floor and brought back a gold ring and a crown from Amphitrite (the goddess of the sea) as proof. Minos's daughter Ariadne fell in love with Theseus. She said, "If you will take me to Athens and marry me, I will tell you the secret of the labyrinth." Theseus agreed. Ariadne gave him a ball of thread. "Tie one end to the entrance of the labyrinth," she said. "Let the thread roll where it will, and it will take you to the Minotaur. When he is asleep at night, you can strangle him. Then follow the thread back to the entrance."

Theseus did as she said. As he approached the Minotaur, it woke up and tried to kill him. They fought, but Theseus was stronger and broke the monster's back.

Successful but bloodied, Theseus staggered out of the maze – but fled before Minos could find out what happened. He abandoned Ariadne, ignoring his promise to her. He also forgot to change the black sails on the boat to white ones. When the boat neared Athens, King Aegeus saw the black sails and thought Theseus had been killed. In grief, Aegeus threw himself into the sea and drowned.

Perseus, the hero
Parents
Perseus's mother was Danae, daughter of King Acrisius of Argos. Danae was locked in a room away from all people for the king had learned that he was destined to be killed by her son. But the god Zeus visited her and she gave birth to Perseus.

Castaways
In fear, Acrisius put Danae and baby Perseus into a chest and cast them into the ocean. A kindly fisherman found them and took them to his home on the island of Seriphos.

Destiny fulfilled
After the Medusa adventure, Perseus returned to Argos. Hearing of his return, Acrisius fled to the city of Larissa. Perseus also went there to compete in some athletic games. By accident, he threw a discus that hit his grandfather and killed him.

Medusa, the monster
Beautiful maiden transformed
According to a Roman myth, Medusa was once a beautiful maiden and was admired by many suitors. She was a priestess in the temple of Athena. Poseidon, the sea god, visited her in the temple. This offended Athena and, in anger, Athena transformed Medusa's golden hair into serpents and made her face look so terrible that onlookers would be turned into stone.

In one version of the myth, Perseus rescued Andromeda by using Medusa's severed head to turn the terrifying sea monster into stone.

Perseus and Medusa

Polydectes, the evil king of Seriphos, wanted to marry the beautiful lady Danae, but her son Perseus protected her. So Polydectes **tricked** Perseus into attempting an impossible task to get rid of him.

A feast was held at the court of Polydectes. All the guests brought gifts for their king – everyone except Perseus who, as the king already knew, was too poor to buy one. In shame, Perseus promised that he would get the king anything he requested.

"Bring me the head of the Gorgon Medusa," challenged Polydectes.

The Gorgons were three fearsome, scaly monsters, who had snakes for hair. The eldest was called Medusa. Anyone who looked at her face turned into stone.

Perseus accepted the challenge and prepared for the journey. Looking down from Mount Olympus, Zeus sent the goddess Athena and god Hermes to help his son. They gave him the shiniest shield and the sharpest sickle in the world.

Following their advice, Perseus set off first to visit the nymphs of the North Wind. These female spirits lent him some winged sandals, a leather bag, and the Cap of Invisibility, belonging to Hades, the god of the underworld.

Wearing the winged sandals and the Cap of Invisibilty, Perseus flew unseen to the far west where he found the Gorgons' cave. They were asleep, so quietly and steathily he approached them. He passed the stony statues of other warriors, who had previously tried to kill them. Looking only at Medusa's reflection in the shiny shield, he cut off her head with a single swipe of the sharp sickle and put it quickly into the leather bag.

Swiftly, he raced out of the cave and leapt into the air before Medusa's sisters could grasp him.

As Perseus flew home, he saw a princess named Andromeda, chained to a rock. Her parents had angered Poseidon, the sea god. The god had sent a terrifying sea monster to destroy their kingdom. The only way to stop the creature was to offer their daughter as a sacrifice.

As the huge monster rose from the waves, Perseus took Medusa's head out of the bag and held it up. The monster looked at the face and was turned into stone. Perseus then married Andromeda before continuing on his journey back to Seriphos.

While Perseus had been away, King Polydectes had forced Danae to serve him. He was shocked and surprised when Perseus appeared.

"Where's my gift?" Polydectes demanded.

Without a word, Perseus held up the head of Medusa and turned the king and his court into stone. Once more he was reunited with his mother. He gave the head of Medusa to the goddess Athena, and she carried it on her shield.

Pegasus, the winged horse
Myths vary about whether the winged horse Pegasus sprang from Medusa's dead body or from drops of blood that fell from her head as Perseus left the cave. Another myth tells how a boy named Bellerophon tamed Pegasus, using Athena's bridle, and rode on him to fight the fearsome Chimera.

Trojan war

Considered to be one of the greatest battles in ancient history, we know about the ten-year long Trojan war from two epic poems, the **Iliad** by the Greek author **Homer** and **The Aeneid** by the Roman poet **Vigil**. The poems tell of great heroics, tragic deaths, and the **destruction** of the great city of Troy.

Agamemnon
King of Mycenae and brother of Menelaus
He was the Commander-in-chief of the Greek forces – a fleet of over 1,000 ships with over 100,000 men.

The Greeks

The Greeks were supported by the gods Poseidon, Athena, Hera, Hermes, and Hephaestus.

The golden apple
At a feast held by Zeus, the uninvited guest Eris, the goddess of discord, appeared and presented a golden apple, with an inscription that read "to the fairest". The three goddesses, Hera, Athena, and Aphrodite, each believed they should receive it. Zeus chose Paris of Troy to judge them. Paris chose Aphrodite, who promised him the most beautiful woman in the world as his wife – Helen, wife of the King of Sparta. This contest caused the start of the Trojan war.

Menelaus
King of Sparta and husband of Helen
He agreed to settle the war by single combat with Paris, but Aphrodite saved Paris and Athena caused the war to continue.

Achilles
Leader of the Myrmidons
He argued with Agamemnon so withdrew from the fighting for much of the conflict. He died when Paris's arrow guided by the god Apollo wounded him in the heel, his only weak spot.

Odysseus (also known as Ulysses)
King of Ithaca
He was a great fighter *(see pages 50–53)* and very resourceful and cunning. He came up with the idea of the wooden horse.

Ajax the Great
King of Salamis
Very tall and strong, Ajax killed many Trojan lords and fought twice with Hector, but didn't succeed in killing him because Hector was protected by some gods.

Patroclus
Friend of Achilles
While Achilles was sulking, Patroclus put on the armour of Achilles and led Achilles's men into battle, but was killed by Hector.

The Trojans

The Trojans were supported by the gods Aphrodite, Apollo, Artemis, and Ares.

KING PRIAM OF TROY MARRIED HECUBA. THEY HAD MANY CHILDREN INCLUDING HECTOR, PARIS, CASSANDRA, AND HELENUS.

King Priam
King of Troy
He was said to have had 50 sons and 50 daughters and many of them are mentioned in myths.

Hecuba
Queen of Troy
When she was a child, she dreamed that she would give birth to a child who would set Troy on fire.

Helen of Troy
Wife of Menelaus, and daughter of Zeus and Leda
She went with Paris to Troy and is known as the face that launched a thousand ships.

Paris
Prince of Troy
He fell in love with Helen and brought her to Troy. He was killed by a poisoned arrow.

Hector
Eldest son of Priam
He was Commander-in-chief of the Trojan forces and was killed by Achilles in revenge for the death of Patroclus.

Aeneas
A Dardanian hero and son of Aphrodite
He escaped after the fall of Troy and his story continues in the Roman epic poem, the *Aeneid*.

Cassandra
Princess of Troy
She could prophesy the future, but due to a curse from Apollo no one believed her warnings.

Helenus
Son of Priam and seer
In the final days of the war, he told the Greeks the secret of how Troy could be destroyed.

Sarpedon and Glaucus
Cousins and leaders of the Lycians
Sarpedon was killed by Patroclus. Glaucus met the Greek warrior Diomedes on the battlefield but as their grandfathers were friends, they chose not to fight each other and instead exchanged armour.

The wooden horse
To end the war, the Greeks built a huge wooden horse and hid 30 soldiers inside. They then pretended to sail away. The Trojans, believing that they had won and this was a victory gift, took the horse into their city. That night, the Greek men crept out of the horse and opened the gates so the rest of the Greek army could enter, and destroyed the city.

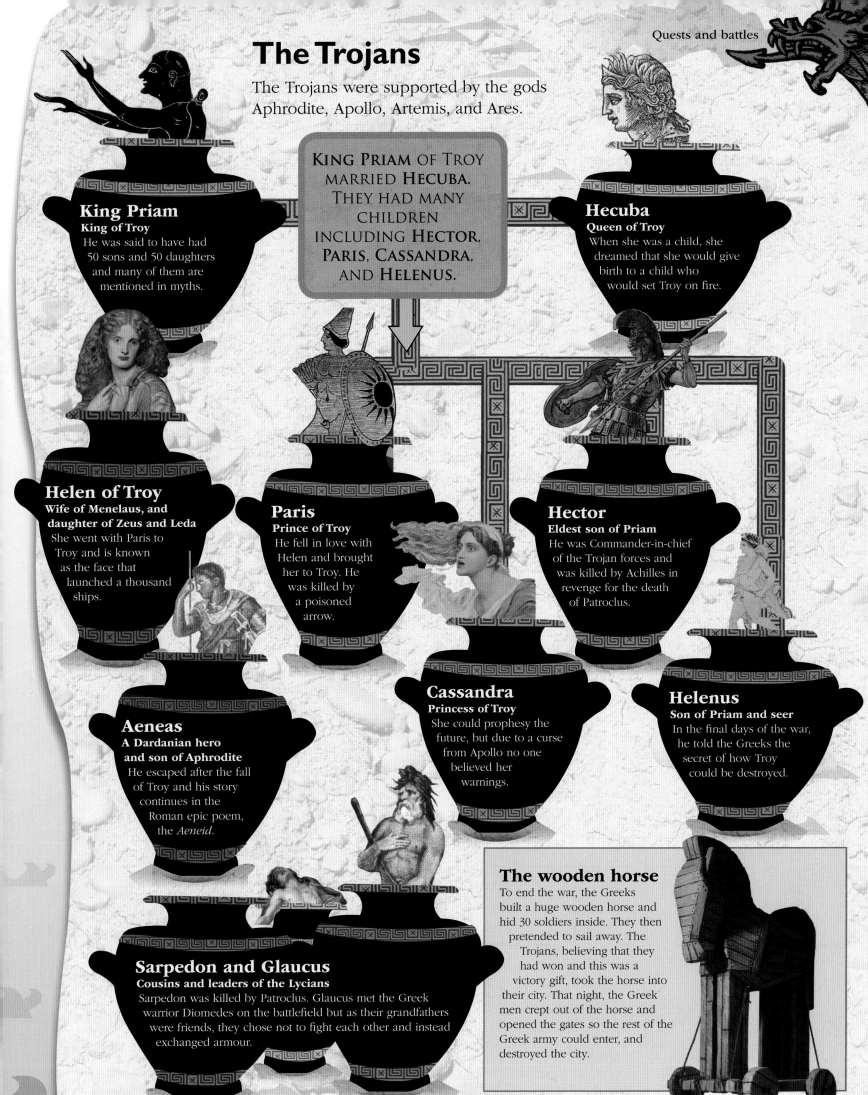

Jason was raised by a wise centaur (half man half horse) called Chiron.

Setting the scene
Childhood

Iolkos was ruled by a good king called Aeson until his power-hungry half-brother Pelias took the throne. But Aeson had a son, Jason – he was the rightful heir, so his mother knew he was in mortal danger and sent him away to be raised by a centaur.

The lost shoe

When Jason came of age, he set out for Iolkos to claim his throne. He had to cross a river, and on the bank, he saw an old woman, too frightened to cross. Jason lifted her onto his back and set out for the other side. The current was strong, though, and when he reached the other side, he was exhausted, and one of his shoes had been lost in the water.

As he helped the old woman down, he stared at her in wonder – she was the goddess Hera, who had put him through this test. As a result of Jason's kindness, the goddess offered him her help whenever she was needed.

Jason and the golden fleece

Long ago, in the kingdom of Iolkos, there was a cruel king named Pelias, who had seized the throne from his brother. He ruled his people harshly, but he lived in fear – a soothsayer had **forseen** that he would be overthrown by a man wearing one shoe!

One day, his brother's son arrived at court to claim the throne. King Pelias was terrified – the youth, who was called Jason, wore only one shoe because he had lost the other on his journey. Disguising his intention to hold onto power, Pelias suggested that Jason complete a special task that would prove him a worthy king. "In the kingdom of Colchis, there is a golden fleece that was stolen from its owner by Aietes, the king. Bring me that golden fleece." Of course, Pelias was lying – the fleece belonged to Aietes.

Fired by duty and the prospect of glory, Jason sought out a company of brave warriors, and had a fabulous ship built for their voyage. The ship was called the Argo, and Jason's warriors were the Argonauts. They had a long and dangerous journey before them, but their leader was strong and their purpose was a noble one.

On the way, they stopped to rescue a blind prophet called Phineus from the Harpies – horrible winged women. In gratitude, Phineus revealed to Jason the secret of passing through the fearsome Clashing Rocks that guarded the route to Colchis. These rocks slammed together to crush any ship that sailed between them. "As you approach," advised the old man, "release a dove into the sky". Jason followed his suggestion. As the bird flew between the rocks, they crashed together, but the creature escaped. Then, when the rocks parted again,

the Argo was able to slip through.

Eventually, the ship arrived in Colchis, and Jason presented himself to Aietes to claim the fleece. Rather than take on the Argonauts, the king agreed to hand over the prize only if Jason demonstrated his strength and courage by carrying out another (seemingly impossible) task. This was to harness two fire-breathing bulls, then plough and sow a field with dragons' teeth – each would grow into a fierce warrior. But meanwhile, Aietes' daughter Medea had fallen in love with Jason. Medea was a sorceress, and she promised to help Jason if he married her, which he did.

Together, they tamed the bulls and defeated the dragons, but Aietes still wouldn't give up the fleece, which was guarded by a deadly serpent. Following Medea's suggestion, Jason played music to lull the serpent to sleep, and captured the prize.

Jason and Medea set sail for Iolkos, and after many more adventures, they arrived safely. Jason claimed his throne, and they ruled for many years.

The special fleece

Long ago, Athamas, ruler of Sicily, left his wife Nephele for a younger woman. Afraid for her children, a boy, Phryxus, and a girl, Helle, Nephele prayed to Zeus for help, so he sent her a flying golden ram to carry them to safety. With the frightened children holding tightly onto its back, the ram flew east, across the water between Europe and Asia. Tragically, Helle lost her grip and fell into the sea. (For thousands of years, this water was called the Hellespont in her honour – today, it's the Dardanelles.) With Phryxus on his back, the ram flew on until it landed in Colchis.

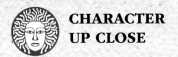
Biography
Oedipus

Family connections
Oedipus's father was Laius and his mother was Jocasta, king and queen of the city of Thebes. A prophecy said Oedipus would kill his father and marry his mother. Frightened, his parents left him to die on a mountainside.

Oedipus was found by shepherds and brought up by Polybus and Merope, king and queen of Corinth.

What's in a name?
Oedipus's name means "swollen feet" as he was abandoned with his feet tied together.

On the road
When Oedipus heard about the prophecy he left home. On his travels he had an argument with a stranger and killed him. Unknowingly he had fulfilled the first part of the prophecy; the stranger was Laius.

A hero's welcome
After Oedipus defeated the Sphinx, the people of Thebes made him their new king. (Their king was mysteriously killed on the road by a stranger.) He married their widowed queen, and again, unknowingly, fulfilled the second part of the prophecy as the queen was his mother, Jocasta.

Oedipus, the tragic hero

Oedipus is the classic ancient Greek tragic hero. Abandoned as a child to prevent a **prophecy** from the Delphi Oracle from coming true, he spent his whole life trying to do the right thing, only to find that he could not change his **fate**.

Ask the Oracle

The Delphi Oracle was a priestess at the Temple of Apollo in ancient Greece. Legend said that rising vapours made her go into a trance and see visions; her fortune-telling was sought by many for centuries. Recently earthquake faults that release potent gases have been found under the temple.

The truth is out

Many years after Oedipus was made king of Thebes, a plague struck the city. The Delphi Oracle said that to save the city, the murderer of the previous king, Laius, had to leave. Oedipus searched for the killer until the blind prophet Tiresias told him the truth. It was Oedipus himself! In shame, Jocasta his wife and mother killed herself, and Oedipus put out his own eyes and was exiled. He died at Colonnus, an entrance to the underworld.

Oedipus's daughter, Antigone goes with him into exile.

The Sphinx terrorized the citizens of Thebes, eating those who couldn't answer her riddle.

The riddle

Q: What has 4 legs in the morning, 2 legs in the day, and 3 legs in the evening?

The Sphinx had a lion's body, wings, and a woman's head.

A: A person. (As a child you crawl on all fours; as a man you walk upright; and as an old man, you walk with a stick – your third leg.)

Oedipus was the only one ever to have defeated the Sphinx.

Oedipus was hailed as a champion by the people of Thebes.

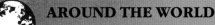
Dragons

Every continent has its tales of **fearsome**, scaly, serpent-like creatures – the test of bravery for many a hero. The evil, fire-breathing, flying dragons of the West often guarded **treasure**. However, the more snake-like Asian dragons were generally just and fair, bringing good **fortune**.

▲ **Heraldic dragon, Europe** Dragons are used on many coats of arms throughout Europe to symbolize strength and authority.

◀ **Ryu, Japan** The three-clawed Japanese dragon lives beneath the sea and controls the rain and stormy weather. It bestows wishes to those brave enough to seek it, which is perhaps why many Zen temples are adorned with dragon images and the Japanese character for "dragon" appears in many temple names.

▲ **La Vouivre, France** Also called Guivre or Wyvern, these dragons fought with their two clawed feet, balancing themselves with their tail.

◀ **Kuh Billaur, Persia
(Present-day Iran)** Here, brave Ali
heroically kills a serpent dragon, Kuh
Billaur, piercing it with his sword.
Dragons were feared throughout
the Middle East. In ancient times, a
dragon was said to have swallowed
the Moon when a lunar eclipse
occurred. People would make loud
noises with cans and bells to get
the dragon to release the Moon.

▼ **Xiuhcoatl Aztecs** In one myth,
the Earth goddess Coatlicue, gave birth
to a warrior called Huitzilopochtli. His
siblings tried to kill him, but he killed
them with the fire serpent Xiuhcoatl
(which means "turquoise snake").

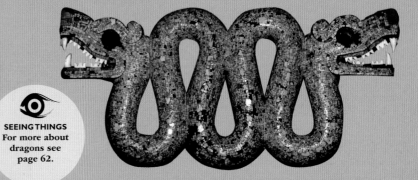

SEEING THINGS
For more about
dragons see
page 62.

▼ **Basilisk, Europe** Reputed to kill with a single glance, the basilisk
(also called a cockatrice) was born from a chicken's egg and hatched on
dung of a toad. In medieval myths, it was often used to symbolize the devil.

▲ **Fafnir, Norse/Germany** In many northern
European myths, dragons were a symbol of greed. Fafnir
was originally a dwarf, son of dwarf king Hreidmar, He
was turned into a dragon when he greedily tried to steal
his father's treasure. He was eventually killed by Sigurd
(known in Germany as Siegfried – *see page 94*).

Beowulf and Grendel the ogre

The longest and best of all Anglo-Saxon epic poems, ***Beowulf*** is set in Denmark during the sixth century. The main part of the story involves the reign of **Hrothgar**, a strong and well-loved king who built a great mead hall called **Heorot** for his court and his warriors. (Mead is an ancient wine made from honey.)

The original poem was written in Old English sometime between the 8th and early 11th centuries. The writer is unknown.

Beowulf the poem
The original
The original poem is very, very long, having 3,182 lines. Before the main section, there's a detailed history of the Danish royal family dating right back to ancient myths.

The story continues...
After Beowulf killed Grendel's mother, the poem describes how he returned to the grateful Hrothgar and shared a final celebration before returning to Geatland.

King of Geatland
Beowulf was made king of Geatland. He ruled wisely and peacefully for 50 years before he faced his final challenge – fighting a ferocious dragon that was furious because some of its treasure had been stolen.

Death of a hero
Although Beowulf killed the dragon, he was badly wounded in the battle, and lay dying. With his last strength, Beowulf asked to be cremated in a huge funeral pyre. High on a cliff by the sea, his ashes were buried along with the dragon's treasure.

For many years, an ogre called Grendel tormented the ageing king, breaking into Heorot at night and killing Hrothgar's warriors (called thanes). Huge and horrible, this monster inspired terror in even these strong, brave men.

When he was young, Hrothgar had helped a warrior from nearby Geatland to settle a feud. Eventually news of Hrothgar's plight reached the warrior's son Beowulf.

Beowulf set out for Heorot with his finest men to help the king, and to build his own reputation for bravery and strength. When Beowulf arrived, Hrothgar organized a huge celebration in the hall. When the feast was over, the Danes went away to sleep in a safe place, and Beowulf and his men kept watch. Soon, the monster burst in, killing one of the Geats before attacking their leader.

After a ferocious struggle, Beowulf ripped Grendel's arm off at the shoulder. Horribly wounded, the ogre escaped to his cave at the bottom of a pool, where he died.

To mark his victory, Beowulf hung up the bloody arm for everyone to see.

The next day, Hrothgar held another great feast to mark the victory, and that night everyone – Danes and Geats – settled down for a peaceful rest.

Later, in the darkness, Grendel's mother broke into Heorot looking for revenge. After retrieving her son's arm, she killed one of the sleeping Danes and escaped to the hidden cave. When Beowulf woke up and discovered what she'd done, he followed her footsteps to the edge of the pool and dived in. But before he reached the bottom, the murderous woman attacked him and dragged him to the dark, damp cave where her son's body lay. Attacking Beowulf with a knife, she struggled hard, but he overpowered and killed her.

Before he left the cave, he cut the head off Grendel's body. Taking it with him as a trophy, he escaped from the cave and made his way back to Heorot.

Beowulf, the dragon slayer
One day, a thief stole from the treasure-trove of a fiery dragon. The furious creature terrorized the countryside, his breath burning fields and homes. Beowulf (now king), with a few of his best men, set off to kill the monster.

When they found him, the king took out his sword and attacked, but the dragon was too strong. All the men fled, except one, Wiglaf, who stayed with Beowulf. After a bloody fight, the dragon was dead, but the king lay dying too. For his bravery, Wiglaf was made the new king.

MAKE YOUR OWN BATTLE SHIELD

Cut out a large shield shape from a piece of cardboard. Make some handles from two strips of cardboard – bend the ends and use strong tape to attach them to the back of the shield. Then decorate the front of the shield.

Paint your shield dark blue or black. To make the gold cross, use two strips of wide gold masking tape.

121

The Knights of the Round Table

In the mid-12th century, stories began being told about **King Arthur** – a British warrior chief thought to have ruled in the late 5th and early 6th centuries. These fantastical stories made him, his knights, and his court into a **magical romantic legend**.

King Arthur
Son of Uther Pendragon
He carried a sword called Excalibur, defeating enemies in many battles, but was killed at Camlann.

Merlin the wizard tells his story to his master Blaise, from l'Histoire de Merlin, *c.1280-90*

Camelot
The fictional turreted castle Camelot became the legendary capital of King Arthur's kingdom. There he reigned with his beautiful queen, Guinevere. Guided by a wise magician called Merlin, he and his chivalrous knights overcame supernatural enemies, such as his evil half sister, the sorceress Morgan le Fay.

Quest for the Holy Grail
In the Arthurian legends, the knights went on many quests to test their bravery and honesty. One of these was the quest for the Holy Grail – the dish that Jesus used at the Last Supper and was said to have magical powers and could cure all illnesses. Many knights tried and failed to find its whereabouts. Only three succeeded but Sir Galahad was the only one who was pure enough to look upon the grail, before being lifted up to heaven.

This tapestry by Edward Burne-Jones shows Sir Bors and Sir Percival being prevented from entering the Grail Chapel, and only Sir Galahad gazes upon the dish.

The Round Table

To keep the peace between his knights, King Arthur built a Round Table so that all would be seen as equal. Medieval stories described the Round Table as having more than 50 seats and every knight vowed to follow a strict code of honour and service.

Sir Galahad
Son of Lancelot
He was a good and handsome knight who succeeded in the quest of the Holy Grail.

In the late 13th century, a Round Table was made, showing 25 seats. It now hangs in the Great Hall in Winchester, UK.

Sir Lancelot du Lac
One of the most famous and skilful knights, who caused the end of Camelot due to his love for Queen Guinevere.

Sir Mordred
Nephew of King Arthur
Later known as the illegitimate son of King Arthur, he turned traitor and fought against the king at the battle of Camlann where he and Arthur were killed.

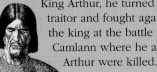

Sir Bors de Ganis
Cousin of Lancelot
He was the only one to survive the quest for the Holy Grail.

Sir Gawain
Nephew of King Arthur
A loyal and brave knight who accepted the challenge of the Green Knight.

Sir Bedivere
One of the main companions of King Arthur, who fought the giant living on Mont St. Michel and, after the king's death, returned Excalibur to the Lady of the Lake.

Sir Tristram de Lyones
This noble knight is known for his love for Isolde due to drinking a love potion when he was escorting her from Ireland to marry a king of Cornwall.

Sir Kay
Foster brother of King Arthur
He was one of the most trusted knights and was in charge of the royal household.

123

Elixir of life

The **desire** to find the secret of staying youthful has been the quest for many a mythical hero and legendary explorer. Throughout history, people have sought the **legendary elixir** – the substance that could give eternal life and total wisdom.

◄ Bimini,

Caribbean A mythical land of plenty and wealth, thought to be somewhere in the Gulf of Honduras, is a location for a magical spring. In the 16th century, the local people told the European explorers, such as Juan Ponce de León, that the water could make them young again.

▲ Emerald Tablet, Ancient Egypt/Greece
The ancient Greek god Hermes and the ancient Egyptian god Thoth were the gods of writing and magic. They were combined into a single god in the late 4th century BCE named Hermes Trismegistus. According to legend, it was this god who wrote the instructions that revealed how to make the elixir known as the Emerald Tablet.

► Philosophers Stone, Medieval India This legendary substance was said to be able to change metals, such as lead, into gold and was also believed to be the elixir of life. Creating this mixture by mixing and heating chemicals occupied the work of many alchemists – scientists who followed ancient philosophy – across Asia, Arabia, and Europe throughout history.

◀ **Amrita,** **Ancient India**
A short-tempered sage, Durvasa, who was an incarnation of Lord Shiva *(see page 99)* became angry with the Hindu gods. He put a curse on them, causing them to lose their immortality. This meant they needed to drink amrita, a milky liquid churned up in the ocean by their enemies, the Asuras, to stay immortal.

▼ **Golden Apples,**
Ancient Greece The Garden of Hesperides in ancient Greek myths had a tree of golden apples that if eaten gave immortality. A hundred-headed serpent that never slept guarded the tree. The Greek gods did not eat these but drank ambrosia to stay immortal.

SEEING THINGS
For more about rabbits in myths see page 102.

◀ **Jade Rabbit,** **China** The Chinese goddess of the Moon, Chang-e, was lonely on the Moon so the Jade Rabbit, who made elixir, went to live with her. Neither of them grew old. In the autumn, the rabbit can be seen pounding the herbs in its pestle and mortar on the Moon's surface.

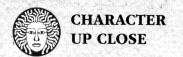
Biography
*Gilgamesh, a
Mesopotamian ruler*

Family connections
*His father was reputedly the
shepherd king Lugalbanda and
his mother was Ninsun, a goddess.*

Superman
*Myths say that Gilgamesh was
part man part god, with
superhuman strength.*

*An ancient stone carving
showing Gilgamesh holding up
the Sun, flanked by two bull men.*

King of Uruk
*Some say Gilgamesh was the
fifth king of Uruk in
Mesopotamia (present-day Iraq),
reigning in 26th century* BCE.

Famous builder
*Gilgamesh was famous for
building the city walls of
Uruk to defend his people.*

A tale of 12 tablets
In the Epic of Gilgamesh,
*Gilgamesh is human rather
than a demi-god. He is also a
tyrannical ruler. His people cry
out to the gods for help, and the
gods create the wild man Enkidu
as a distraction for Gilgamesh.
The two have many adventures
together, including the slaying of
the monster Humbaba and the
great Bull of Heaven. Enkidu
then has a dream that says he
will die because of his role in
slaughtering the beasts.*

*After Gilgamesh's fruitless search
for immortality, he returns to
Uruk. In the last tablet he is
visited by Enkidu from the
underworld.*

Gilgamesh, the tyrant

The story of the **warrior king** Gilgamesh is thought to be one of the first stories ever written. A jumble of ancient broken stone tablets found in the ruins of an Assyrian palace reveal a 4,000-year-old **epic** tale of tyranny, true **friendship**, and the search for immortality.

The search for eternal life

When Enkidu died, Gilgamesh was worried about his own death so he set out to search for the secret of immortality. Utnapishtim, the survivor of a great flood, told him that nothing was permanent. To prove it was impossible to be immortal, Utnapishtim ordered Gilgamesh to stay awake for a week, but Gilgamesh couldn't. Utnapishtim's wife made her husband tell Gilgamesh about a plant that would make him young again. Gilgamesh found it on the seabed, but a serpent ate it before he could, which is why snakes can shed their skins.

Enkidu

Enkidu was a wild man raised by animals. Found by a woman, he was brought to the city of Uruk. Gilgamesh heard of his legendary strength and challenged him to a fight. After the fight the two men became firm friends and inseparable.

Enkidu represents the wild, natural world, whereas Gilgamesh represents the civilized world.

Inseparable

Gilgamesh and Enkidu had many adventures together. On one occasion the goddess Ishtar sent the Bull of Heaven to kill Gilgamesh when he told her he did not love her. Gilgamesh and Enkidu managed to defeat the bull effortlessly.

Enkidu is punished by the gods for his part in killing the bull.

Lost kingdoms

Idyllic kingdoms and powerful civilizations **lost** under the waves of the ocean, destroyed, or hidden in mountains appear in many myths and legends from around the world. People still search today for the **exact locations** and for evidence of their existence, but often only the purest of heart and mind will find them.

◀ **Ys, France** In Brittany, a legend tells of a city built below sea level and protected by a dam. The king kept the keys to the gate of the dam, but his daughter stole them to let her lover into the city. The water flooded the city, killing everyone except the king and a saint.

▼ **Atlantis, Ancient Greece** According to the ancient Greek philosopher Plato, the island of Atlantis was home to the perfect civilization, shaped by Poseidon, the god of the sea, for his bride Clito. All their sons were wise and peaceful kings but, as generations passed, the rulers became greedy and quarrelsome. Shamed, Poseidon stirred up the sea and drowned Atlantis in a tsunami.

▲ **Mu, Pacific Ocean** Sunk beneath the waters of the Pacific Ocean is thought to be a large lost continent. Like Atlantis, it was once the land of a successful civilization, which was dramatically destroyed. Another "lost civilization" is Lemuria, sited somewhere in the Indian or Pacific Oceans.

▲ **Kitezh, Russia** In the 12th century, a town was built on the shores of Lake Sveltloyar in Russia. When Mongols attacked the defenceless town, the people just prayed and then fountains of water burst from the ground and the town sank into the lake. According to legend, only those pure in heart and soul can see the town and hear singing under the water.

▲ **Shambhala (Shangri-la), Tibet**
Hidden somewhere in the Kunlan Mountains of the Himalayas is an earthly paradise. This Tibetan mythical kingdom is thought to look like a lotus with eight petals and is where only the very holiest of people live.

▲ **Hawaiki, Polynesia** The Maoris of New Zealand believe their ancestors arrived in canoes from a mythical island in the Pacific Ocean. They believe that when they die, their spirits return to this place, but no one knows exactly where it is.

▶ **Seven Cities of Gold,**
Americas Quivira and Cibola are two of the seven cities that according to myth were founded by seven bishops who fled southern Spain when the African-Arabian people invaded. When the Spanish explorers travelled to Central and South America, they heard stories of seven cities made of gold and full of riches. They thought these were the cities of their seven bishops.

*Made by the **Muisca** people, this solid-gold sculpture depicts the ancient ritual on Lake Guatavita.*

Eternal search

Expeditions

Over the centuries, people have searched for El Dorado all across South America, not only in Ecuador, Peru, Mexico, and Venezuela, but also along the Amazon and Orinoco rivers. One explorer – Francisco Vazquez de Coronado – even travelled as far as Kansas in the US to seek the legendary city.

Lake Guatavita

Most experts agree though, that the inspiration for El Dorado is Lake Guatavita, and many adventurers have tried to prove it. At the end of the 16th century, forty years after early Spaniards picked up bits of gold around the shore, a Spanish merchant dug a huge notch in the lake's rim in order to lower the water. This worked – but the cut collapsed, killing hundreds of workmen.

Tantalizing treasure

In 1911, an English gold company used a complex set of tunnels to empty the water, but the muddy bottom hardened instantly. A few gold items were recovered, but the lake refilled quickly, and the company had to auction everything they found to cover their costs.

Tantalizingly, in 1968, in a lakeside cave, walkers found a solid gold miniature of the original El Dorado, with his attendants, on his raft, setting out to offer treasure to the gods in the lake (see above). This extraordinary treasure is in the Gold Museum in the city of Bogota, Columbia.

City of gold (El Dorado)

"Over the Mountains of the Moon, Down the Valley of the Shadow, Ride, **boldly ride…** If you seek for **El Dorado**."

In 1849, American writer Edgar Allan Poe hinted at the location of El Dorado, the mythical, long-lost city of gold in South America. But originally, the name "El Dorado" referred to a person, not a place.

The story began in the northern Andes mountains of Colombia, among the Muisca people. Whenever a new chief came to the throne, he made a pilgrimage to Lake Guatavita to make offerings to the gods. When he got to the water's edge, his clothes were removed, and he was completely covered in gold dust. As he sat on a wooden raft with his attendants, servants surrounded him with objects made from more gold and precious stones. The raft was then pushed into the lake – when it reached the middle, the treasure was thrown over the edge, and the chief bathed in the lake, so the glittery dust on his skin was washed into the water.

Ancient riches

Muisca people may not have built the city of El Dorado, but like the other tribes in this area, they were rich in natural resources – not only gold, but emeralds, copper, coal, and salt. Gold was so plentiful that they used it in many of their handicrafts as they were skilled goldsmiths. They also produced beautiful textiles and distinctive, brightly coloured pottery.

When the Spaniards arrived during the 16th century, they heard this story, and began talking about the chief as "El Dorado" – the gilded (gold-covered) man. This tale led them to believe there was a fabulously rich city somewhere nearby, and the legend was fuelled by the fact that they actually did find Lake Guatavita, and tried to drain it. They didn't succeed, but they lowered its level enough to reveal hundreds of precious objects along the edge. The search for El Dorado the city had begun.

For years, Spanish explorers hacked through the dense rainforest looking for the golden place. They never found it, and many died in the jungle – of heat, of starvation, of fever, and of deadly diseases carried by mosquitos. Word of El Dorado spread, and other countries joined the search. The English explorer, Sir Walter Raleigh twice sailed to South America looking for gold, and on his second expedition, he took his son, Watt. By this time, Walter was an old man, and he stayed in camp while his son travelled deep into the rainforest. But when Watt arrived at the city, he got into a fight with Spanish treasure hunters, and was killed.

Still today, some people believe there is a city of gold lost in the South American rainforest – always deeper in the jungle, over another mountain, or across the next river. One modern historian remarked, "We believe in El Dorado because we want it to be true".

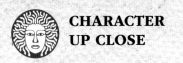
Biography
Robin Hood

The story so far...
Stories about Robin Hood (or Robehood, Rabunbod, Robyn Hude or many similar names) have been around since the 13th century. In some of the early tales (most of which are ballads – folk plays or poems), Robin lived in Yorkshire. In others, he was a peasant, and in still others, he served King Edward. By the end of the 19th century though, the story we're familiar with had become established.

The Robin we know
Robin Hood was born Robert Fitzooth (Robin was a common short form of Robert). He lived in a place called Locksley, and he was a nobleman – the Earl of Huntingdon. Robin and his family were loyal supporters of King Richard the Lionheart, who was away fighting in the Crusades.

The Crusades were medieval campaigns by Christian forces to capture the Holy Lands.

Forces of evil
While the king was away, his wicked brother John seized the throne. John gathered riches by accusing good men of breaking the law, arresting them, and taking their lands and money.

The Sheriff of Nottingham and Sir Guy of Gisborne were corrupt officials acting on behalf of Prince John. They received a share of any wealth they gathered. Robin refused to serve King John, which made him an outlaw.

Robin Hood

One of the most popular of all legendary figures, Robin Hood is the **perfect hero**. He steals from the rich, helps the poor, defends the weak, and stays **loyal** to his rightful king. Over the centuries, there have been many versions of the Robin Hood tale, yet no-one knows for sure if he ever **existed**…

Setting the scene

Robin was an outlaw who lived with his band of Merry Men in Sherwood Forest. A loyal supporter of King Richard, Robin was in hiding from Prince John, Richard's brother, who claimed the throne, and from John's evil friends, the Sheriff of Nottingham and Sir Guy of Gisborne.

Eventually, when King Richard returned from the Crusades, he not only pardoned Robin and his followers (here kneeling in his presence), he later attended the wedding of Robin and Marian.

Robbing the rich

As well as being expert archers, Robin and his men were highly skilled with the sword and staff (a long fighting stick). On the road that ran through their leafy greenwood home, they regularly attacked and robbed King John's wicked nobles – of either weapons or money. The weapons were put to good use by the band, and the money bought supplies for themselves and for the poor.

Cast and crew

With Robin Hood in Sherwood Forest was a large band of followers (about two hundred), but we only have details about the ones who were closest to him. When Richard returned from the Crusades, he was so impressed with the Merry Men that he took them into his service so their loyalty and skill could serve their country.

Maid Marian *As daughter of Lord Fitzwalter, Lady Marian was engaged to Robert Fitzooth (Robin Hood). Their wedding service was underway when Sir Guy arrived to arrest Robin, and the ceremony was interrupted before vows were exchanged. This is why she's called "Maid Marian".*

Much, the miller's son, *was taken in by the outlaws after King John's men killed his father. John ordered this killing because the man had shot a deer in Sherwood Forest (crown property) to feed his hungry family.*

Will Scarlet *was born Will Scathlock, but nicknamed for the russet-red clothes he always wore.*

Little John *was originally called John Little, but renamed with affection for his towering height.*

Friar Tuck *was a small round priest, who was turned out of his abbey by Sir Guy for supporting Robin. Christened Michael Tuck, he was Father Michael until he joined the Merry Men, when he became Friar Tuck.*

Happy ever after

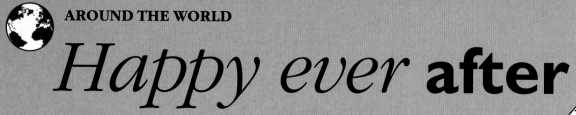

Many cultures believe that the **spirit**, or soul, of a person lives on after **death** in a place called the **afterlife**. Some see it as a place of happiness; others see it as a pale reflection of the living world; and yet others see it as a **place of judgement,** where the good are rewarded by being sent to paradise or punished by being sent to the underworld *(see pages 44–45).*

SEEING THINGS For more about Norse gods see pages 90–91.

▲ **Svarga (or Swarga),** India

Within some Hindu traditions Svarga is a paradise set on Mount Meru. Those who have led good lives but haven't yet achieved perfection live here for a time before they are reincarnated in another life on Earth.

▲ **Valhalla,** Norse

Norsemen that died heroically in battle were taken to Valhalla, Odin's great hall, by the Valkyries (warrior goddesses). Provided with a feast, the warriors waited here, preparing for the day when Odin would call on them to fight their last battle at the end of the world, the battle of the gods – Ragnarok *(see page 93).*

◀ Afterlife, Aztecs

Tlaloc, the rain god, was responsible for those who died by drowning or by disease or illness. He sent these people to a happy afterlife in a garden of Paradise, as shown here in an Aztec wall painting in the ancient Mexican city of Teotihuacan.

◀ Paradise, Aztecs

Aztec women who had died in childbirth, warriors killed on the battlefield, and merchants killed during a journey joined the Sun up in the heavens. After four years of orbiting, they became hummingbirds feeding on the flowers in paradise.

▲ Elysium, Ancient Greece

The Elysian fields were part of Greek underworld (see pages 44–45) where the good and the heroic went to enjoy eternal bliss when they died. Those who had led ordinary lives, neither heroic or very sinful, went to the Asphodel Meadows, where life was dull and boring.

▶ Afterlife, North

America Pueblo Indians believe that the dead either become rainclouds, go to live with the ancestors, or become a spirit called a Kachina.

▲ Aaru, Ancient Egypt When a person died, their

soul was weighed in the underworld, Duat. If the soul weighed exactly the same as the ostrich feather of truth belonging to the goddess of order and justice, Ma'at, then it could go to a place of pleasure called Aaru. Those who made it there were called "eternally living" and were ruled by the god Osiris. Those whose lives were heavy with sin were eaten by the demon Ammit (see page 41).

135

Tell us a story!

Discover the ancient stories and **spread the word** – **become** a storyteller!

Our world is rich in **ancient myths and legends**. They have been **handed down** through countless generations and across the centuries by **storytellers**. Artists have portrayed them in paintings, sculptures, ceramics, costumes, and masks.

Fire your imagination by visiting museums and galleries and national parks and seeing the paintings and sculptures up close.

Explore your local library and find **inspiration** in novels created around famous mythological characters and plots.

Delve into the wealth of stories from **different cultures** by exploring **mythology** from around the world on the internet, in books, and in films.

Using all that you have seen and read, have a go at recreating your favourite myth **in your own words**, using your own pictures or things you have made. Or take a current news event and **retell it with mime** or in a **drama,** so that it is remembered by many in years to come.

You too can be a storyteller and captivate others with your tales, inspiring them to pass the story on to future generations!

The "Mountain Man" storyteller recounts some north American legends at Keystone, Colorado, USA.

Glossary

Deity another name for a god or goddess.

Deluge very heavy rain.

Demi-god a person who is part god and part human.

Demon an evil spirit that torments and causes pain and suffering.

Dreaming, The Australian aborigines believe this is an ongoing time from when the Earth was woken up and the first ancestors created all living things.

Dwarf a mythical race of short humanlike creatures.

Elixir the substance that keeps a person forever young so he never dies.

Embalming treating a dead body (corpse) to stop it from decaying.

Empire a nation that controls other countries by imposing its politics and military.

Enchantress a woman who uses magic and chants spells.

Epic a long poem, describing the adventures of a heroic figure or the exploits of a nation.

Heaven a place where gods and goddesses lived.

Hell a place of everlasting torment and punishment.

Heraldry a system of using symbols relating to a person's family history to decorate a coat-of-arms to use on a flag or a shield.

Hero a character in a story who shows courage and completes brave deeds.

Aborigines the native people of Australia.

Alchemist a person who mixes chemicals, seeking the substance to turn metals into gold and creating elixir to become immortal.

Ancestor a person from whom someone is descended, such as a great, great, great grandfather.

Asuras one of the race of demons who were the enemies of the Indian demi-gods.

Aztecs people of a warrior civilization in central Mexico that was most powerful before the Spanish conquest in the 1500s.

Centaur a creature with a head, arms, and topmost body of a man, and body and legs of a horse.

Chaos the swirling darkness in the beginning before creation.

Chivalrous courageous, considerate, and loyal behaviour, which is particularly associated with knights.

Cornucopia a goat's horn overflowing with fruit, flowers, and corn as a symbol of plenty.

Creation the process of making something exist for the first time.

Culture a way of life in music, arts, literature, and other learning for a particular society

Cyclops a member of a race of one-eyed giants.

Immortal never die so live forever.

Incas people who belonged to a civilization that were living in the central Andes Mountains of South America before the Spanish conquest in the 1500s.

Jultomten a bearer of gifts at Christmas, such as the tomte or nisse of Scandinavian folklore.

Kachina an ancestral spirit of the Hopi and other native American people or a person who represents a spirit in a ceremonial dance.

Labyrinth a maze or a confusing network of paths that make it difficult to work out the right way to go.

Legend a historical story that has been passed down over the years but the facts have been altered and the characters made more or less heroic.

Lunar eclipse when the Moon passes into the shadow of the Earth, so the Sun cannot directly shine on it.

Maori the native people of New Zealand who are descended from the people of the Pacific Islands.

Mayas people from a civilization that existed in southern Mexico, Belize, and Guatemal from 2000 BCE and were most successful between 250-900 CE.

Medieval a period of history in Europe, also called the Middle Ages, between 5th century and 15th century CE.

Mortal will one day die.

Satyr a woodland god with horse's ears and tail in ancient Greek mythology or a god with goat's horns, legs, and tail in Roman mythology.

Myth a traditional story, explaining natural or social events, and often involves supernatural characters.

Norse people of medieval Scandinavian countries.

Nymph a nature spirit.

Oracle a priest or priestess who gave prophecies to those seeking advice from the gods. Also the name of the place or temple where the priest or priestess lived.

Paradise a place of everlasting happiness and contentment.

Pharaoh a ruler in ancient Egypt.

Potion a liquid with magical healing properties.

Prophecy a prediction of the future.

Realm another word for kingdom, an area controlled by a ruler.

Reincarnation the rebirth of a soul into a new body.

Ritual a set of actions done in a set way for religious reasons.

Sacred connected with a god and worthy of respect.

Saga a long story about heroic adventures.

Scandinavia part of northern Europe, including the countries Norway, Finland, Sweden, Denmark, Iceland, and the Faro Islands.

Shaman a person who acts as a go-between of the visible world and an invisible spirit world, using magic and chants.

Shapeshifter a supernatural being that can change forms.

Siren in Greek mythology, a creature with the head of a woman and the wings of a bird, whose singing lures sailors to wreck their ships on rocks.

Soothsayer someone who predicts the future.

Sorceress a woman who has magical powers.

Soul the spiritual part of a human or animal.

Spirit a supernatural being; also the non-physical parts of a person that defines who they are.

Storyteller a person who tells, performs, or writes a story.

Supernatural existing outside the natural visible world with powers that go beyond natural forces.

Superstition a belief in an action or situation that cannot be reasoned and created by the fear of the unknown.

Titans one of the families of giants in ancient Greek mythology.

Trickster a mischievous character who upsets the gods and the balance of natural things.

Trojan people from the ancient city of Troy, thought to have been in north-west Turkey near narrow straits called The Dardenelles.

Underworld the land of the dead.

Vampire a dead person in mythology that rises from its grave at night to find victims and drink their blood by biting them in the neck.

Void emptiness.

Voyage a long journey, usually by sea.

/Xam San an ethnic group connected to the San people of South Africa. The "/" stands for a "click" sound, thought to be left over from the earliest human language.

Index

Acknowledgements

Dorling Kindersley would like to thank Penny Smith for proofreading.

The publisher would like to thank the following for their kind permission to reproduce their photographs:

(Key: a-above; b-below/bottom; c-centre; f-far; l-left; r-right; t-top)

1 Alamy Images: The Art Gallery Collection (bl). **2-3 Hrana Janto**. **4 Alamy Images:** Mary Evans Picture Library. **5 The Bridgeman Art Library:** Private Collection (b). **Dreamstime.com:** Milos Tasic (background). **6 Alamy Images:** Universal Images Group Limited (c). **7 akg-images:** (t). **Adam Vehige:** (b). **Wellcome Images:** (c). **8 Alamy Images:** WoodyStock (bl). **Corbis:** Thomas Francisco (tl). **8-9 Alamy Images:** Mary Evans Picture Library (Kraken). **Corbis:** Michael Busselle (b). **9 Alamy Images:** Patrick Blake (br); Horizon International Images Limited (tr). **Corbis:** Visuals Unlimited (cra). **10-11 akg-images**. **12-13 Getty Images:** LWA (background). **12 The Bridgeman Art Library:** Deir el-Medina, Thebes, Egypt / Giraudon (tl); Private Collection (tr); Horniman Museum, London, UK / Photo © Heini Schneebeli (br). **Werner Forman Archive:** (bl). **13 Alamy Images:** Sebastian (tl). **Maya W. aka "Bloodhound Omega" http://bloodhound-omega.deviantart.com/, Claudia Schmidt aka "AlectorFencer. http://alectorfencer. deviantart.com/:** (c). **14 Alamy Images:** Mary Evans Picture Library (tl). **Dreamstime.com:** Milos Tasic (background). **15 Dreamstime.com:** Milos Tasic (background). **16 Alamy Images:** Mireille Vautier (cl); Mark Wiener (br). **Dreamstime. com:** Splinex (tl). **Hrana Janto:** (bl). **Science Photo Library:** John Chumack (c). **17 Alamy Images:** Eduardo Mariano Rivero. **18 Alamy Images:** Prisma Archivo (br). **18-19 Dreamstime.com:** Milos Tasic (background). **19 The Bridgeman Art Library:** Museum of Fine Arts, Boston, Massachusetts, USA / William Sturgis Bigelow Collection (l). **20 Alamy Images:** Penny Tweedie / © DACS 2011 / DACS, London 2014 (bl); Christine Osborne Pictures (br). **Dreamstime.com:** Ben Goode (cr). **J. Reisinger/jr-teams. com:** (cl). **22 Alamy Images:** Travelscape Images (l). **Dreamstime.com:** Clairev (tl). **Nigel Fish, www. nigelfishphotography.co.uk:** (tr). **23 Alamy Images:** David Wall (family tree). **CGTextures.com:** (panels, bl). **Fotolia:** Sébastien Murat . **24 Alamy Images:** Robin Chittenden (b). **Dreamstime.com:** Splinex (tl). **25 The Bridgeman Art Library:** Private Collection / © Look and Learn (tl). **June Grant:** Matariki Gallery, www.matariki.nl (tr). **NASA:** JPL / NGA (b). **26 Bryan & Cherry Alexander / ArcticPhoto:** (tl). **Dreamstime.com:** Milos Tasic (background). **27 Dreamstime.com:** Rudchenko (br/paper). **Adele Jackson:** (c). **Hrana Janto:** (t, br). **28 Alamy Images:** Michele Burgess (tl). **naturepl.com:** Pete Oxford (bl). **Kellan Stover:** (r). **28-29 Dreamstime.com:** Bjarne Henning Kvaale (background). **30 Alamy Images:** John Takai (tr). **The Bridgeman Art Library:** Museo Casa Diego Rivera (INBA), Guanajuato, Mexico / Index / © 2011 Banco de México Diego Rivera Frida Kahlo Museums Trust, Mexico, D.F. / DACS / DACS, London 2014 (b). **31 Alamy Images:** Mary Evans Picture Library (bl); Suzanne Long (cl); Ivy Close Images (tr); Interfoto (br). **32-33 Alamy Images:** Dennis Cox (family tree). **32 akg-images:** De Agostini Pic.Lib (bc). **Alamy Images:** bilwissedition Ltd. & Co. KG (br); Mary Evans Picture Library (cra); Interfoto (c/hera). **The Bridgeman Art Library:** Louvre, Paris, France (tr); Musee National de la Renaissance, Ecouen, France / Giraudon (cla). **Corbis:** (c/ zeus). **Dreamstime.com:** Clairev (tl). **Getty Images:** The Bridgeman Art Library (cr); DEA / G. Dagli Orti (cl). **The Art Archive:** Archaeological Museum Venice / Collection Dagli Orti (bl). **33 akg-images:** De Agostini Pic.Lib (ca); Electa (c). **Alamy Images:** Mary Evans Picture Library (bl). **Getty Images:** Archive Photos (cl); Superstock (bc); DEA / G. Dagli Orti (br); DEA / G Nimatallah (cb); The Bridgeman Art Library (cr). **The Art Archive:** Archaeological Museum Delphi / Gianni Dagli Orti (t). **34 akg-images:** (br). **Getty Images:** The Bridgeman Art Library (l). **34-35 Dreamstime. com:** Milos Tasic (background). **35 The Bridgeman Art Library:** Private Collection / The Stapleton Collection (tl). **Corbis:** Bettmann (r). **Dreamstime.com:** Rudchenko (tc). **36 Alamy Images:** Ivy Close Images (tr). **Mattias Fahlberg:** (l). **Julie Newdoll, www.brushwithscience.com:** (cr). **37 Alamy Images:** Ancient Art & Architecture Collection Ltd (tl). **The Bridgeman Art Library:** Private Collection / The Stapleton Collection (tr); Private Collection / Archives Charmet (b). **Corbis:** Bettmann (tc). **38 Stencil Kingdom - www.stencilkingdom.com**. **39 The Bridgeman Art Library:** Bibliotheque des Arts Decoratifs, Paris, France / Archives Charmet (tr). **Dreamstime.com:** Rudchenko (cra). **40-41 Corbis:** So Hing-Keung (family tree). **40 The Bridgeman Art Library:** Brooklyn Museum of Art, New York, USA (cl). **Corbis:** The Art Archive (tr/narmer); Charles & Josette Lenars (br/nut). **Dreamstime.com:** Clairev (tr). **Getty Images:** De Agostini (cr); DEA Picture Library (bl). **Wikipedia:** Jeff Dahl (tc). **41 Alamy Images:** Interfoto (br/ book). **Corbis:** Gianni Dagli Orti (cra); Roger Wood (cla/ osiris); Sandro Vannini (background). **Getty Images:** DEA / G. Dagli Orti (tl, bl/horus, cr). **Wikipedia:** Jeff Dahl (tr/seth). **42-43 Alamy Images:** North Wind Picture Archives (b). **42 Alamy Images:** The Art Gallery Collection (tc). **Corbis:** Christie's Images (l). **43 Alamy Images:** Mary Evans Picture Library (br). **The Bridgeman Art Library:** Private Collection / The Stapleton Collection (tr). **Dreamstime.com:** Rudchenko (crb). **44 Alamy Images:** The Art Gallery Collection (l). **The Bridgeman Art Library:** Ancient Art and Architecture Collection Ltd. (cr). **Corbis:** Historical Picture Archive (tr). **45 Alamy Images:** Mary Evans Picture Library (tl); Lordprice Collection (bl); The Print Collector (br). **The Bridgeman Art Library:** Museo de Antropologia, Jalapa, Mexico / Photo © Boltin Picture Library (tr). **46-47 Wellcome Images**. **48-49 Corbis:** Glowimages (background); Marie Hickman (background 2). **48 akg-images:** (tl). **Alamy Images:** Mary Evans Picture Library (bl); Ivy Close Images (tr). **The Bridgeman Art Library:** Private Collection / The Stapleton Collection (br). **49 Alamy Images:** Pictorial Press Ltd (r). **The Bridgeman Art Library:** Private Collection / Photo © O. Vaering (bl). **Mary Evans Picture Library:** (tl). **50 akg-images:** (cr). **Alamy Images:** Rupert Hansen (cl). **The Bridgeman Art Library:** Gallery Oldham, UK (t). **51 The Bridgeman Art Library:** Bibliotheque des Arts Decoratifs, Paris, France / Archives Charmet. Circe, 1911 (colour litho), Edmund Dulac, permission granted by Hodder Children's Books, a division of Hachette Children's Books, 338 Euston Road,London NW1 3BH / Hodder Children's Books, a division of Hachette Children's Books, 338 Euston Road,London NW1 3BH. **52 Alamy Images:** Lebrecht Music and Arts Photo Library (tl). **53 Dreamstime.com:** Rudchenko (br/paper). **Mary Evans Picture Library:** (bl). **54 Alamy Images:** The Art Gallery Collection (tr); Mary Evans Picture Library (tl). **The Bridgeman Art Library:** Private Collection / Photo © O. Vaering (bl/, nokken, br). **55 Corbis:** Asian Art & Archaeology, Inc. (bl). **Mattias Fahlberg:** (r). **Mary Evans Picture Library:** (cl). **National Gallery Of Victoria, Melbourne:** Danny Nalorlman Djorlom, Kunwinjku c.1952–2005, The killing of Lumaluma 1988, earth pigments on Stringybark 65.5 x 172.0 cm. Gift of Penny Blazey, 1989. (c) Estate of the artist 2011 licensed by Aboriginal Artists Agency (AAA) / Aboriginal Artists Agency Ltd (tr). **56 Alamy Images:** bilwissedition Ltd. & Co. KG (bl). **Dreamstime.com:** Splinex (tl). **Getty Images:** The Bridgeman Art Library (tr). **56-57 Mattias Fahlberg**. **58 Alamy Images:** Paul Moore (clb). **Dreamstime.com:** Milos Tasic (background); Rudchenko (bl); Daniel Wiedemann (br). **59 Dreamstime. com:** Noel Powell (b). **Brad Heyd:** (br). **Island Art Publishers:** Thunderbird and Killer Whale, by Joe Wilson (c). **60 Alamy Images:** North Wind Picture Archives. **61 akg-images:** British Library (tl). **Alamy Images:** The Art Gallery Collection (bl); North Wind Picture Archives (l/ background); directphoto.bz (cr). **The Bridgeman Art Library:** Private Collection / © Look and Learn (tr). **62 Alamy Images:** Digifoto (tc/red lanterns, tr/red lanterns); Jade57 (l, br); photonic 2 (tc). **Werner Forman Archive:** (cr). **63 Alamy Images:** Argus Photo (c); TAO Images Ltd (ca, cl); Wendy Connett (bc); Jade57 (br); Best View Stock (cr); Digifoto (t/red lanterns, tr, tl/red lanterns); photonic 2 (t/ rabbit lantern). **Corbis:** Historical Picture Archive (tl). **64-65 Teddy Edmund Tan Pavon, http://lagunapavon. deviantart.com**;. **Teddy Edmund Tan Pavon, http:// lagunapavon.deviantart.com**;. **64-65 Teddy Edmund Tan Pavon, http://lagunapavon.deviantart.com**;. **Teddy Edmund Tan Pavon, http://lagunapavon.deviantart.com**;. **64 Tu Bui, www.ArtofTu.com:** (bl). **Dreamstime.com:** Drizzd (tl). **66-67 Allen Douglas, www. allendouglasstudio.com**. **66 The Bridgeman Art Library:** Private Collection / Paul Freeman (tl). **Jisuk Cho:** (tr). **67 The Bridgeman Art Library:** Private Collection (tr); Private Collection / Dinodia (br); Royal Library, Copenhagen, Denmark (c). **Ebert Naves:** (tl). **68 Dreamstime.com:** Dr.alex (br). **Photo SCALA, Florence:** © 2011. Image copyright The Metropolitan Museum of Art / Art Resource (bl). **69 Dreamstime.com:** Siloto (bl); Lianquan Yu (br). **70 The Bridgeman Art Library:** Manchester Art Gallery, UK. **70-71 Dreamstime.com:** Milos Tasic (background). **71 akg-images:** (tr). **The Bridgeman Art Library:** Bibliotheque des Arts Decoratifs, Paris, France / Archives Charmet (b). **72 Alamy Images:** Universal Images Group Limited (tl); Wildlife GmbH (tc). **naturepl.com:** Phil Savoie (r). **Photolibrary:** Tsuneo Nakamura (br). **Science Photo Library:** K Jayaram (cb). **73 The Bridgeman Art Library:** National Gallery, London (tr). **Photolibrary:** Heiner Heine / imagebroker.net (cl). **74 Dreamstime.com:** Lana Langlois (c). **Fotolia:** Scott Maxwell (r, l). **The Art Archive:** Bibliothèque Municipale Dijon / Gianni Dagli Orti (t). **75 akg-images:** (r); British Library (l). **Dreamstime.com:** Rudchenko (tr). **76 Alamy Images:** Michael Philip (b). **Dreamstime.com:** Splinex (tl). **Mary Evans Picture Library:** (bl, t). **77 Mattias Fahlberg**. **Fotolia**. **78 The Bridgeman Art Library:** Private Collection / Archives Charmet (tr). **Corbis:** Stapleton Collection (br). **Allen Douglas, www.allendouglasstudio.com:** (l). **Mary Evans Picture Library:** Medici (b). **79 akg-images:** (tr). **Alamy Images:** Melba Photo Agency (bl). **The Bridgeman Art Library:** Private Collection (tl); Private Collection / Photo © The Maas Gallery, London (crb). **Mary Evans Picture Library:** Medici (br, t). **80 Dorling Kindersley:** Bedrock Studios (b). **Dreamstime.com:** Splinex (tl). **State Library Of Victoria, Melbourne:** (c). **81 Allen Douglas, www. allendouglasstudio.com:** (t). **Getty Images:** Mike Kowalski (bl); Visuals Unlimited, Inc. / Dave Watts (br). **82-83 Dreamstime.com:** Milos Tasic (background). **John Wigley**. **82 The Art Archive:** Bibliothèque des Arts Décoratifs Paris / Gianni Dagli Orti (tl, tc). **83 Chrissie Graboski:** (br). **84-85 akg-images**. **84 Alamy Images:** RTimages (bl). **Corbis:** Studio Eye (cla). **Dreamstime.com:** Splinex (tl). **85 Alamy Images:** JTB Photo Communications, Inc. (tl). **86-87 Adam Vehige**. **88 Alamy Images:** Lebrecht Music and Arts Photo Library (tr). **The Bridgeman Art Library:** Palazzo Ducale, Mantua, Italy (br). **Kamil Jadczak:** (l). **89 Alamy Images:** Mary Evans Picture Library (cl, br); World History Archive (bl). **Mattias Fahlberg:** (tr). **Getty Images:** The Bridgeman Art Library (tl). **90 Dreamstime.com:** Clairev (tl). **Jemma Westing**. **91 akg-images:** IAM (tr, ca); ullstein bild (tl). **Alamy Images:** Classic Image (br); Ivy Close Images (family tree); Robert Adrian Hillman (cla); Mary Evans Picture Library (clb). **The Bridgeman Art Library:** Royal Library, Copenhagen, Denmark (c). **Dreamstime.com:** Rudchenko (cra). **Mary Evans Picture Library:** (cb, bl). **92 akg-images:** (r). **Dreamstime.com:** Artaniss8 (t); Splinex (tl). **TopFoto.co.uk:** The Granger Collection (cla, bl). **93 Alamy Images:** Interfoto (br). **Getty Images:** The Bridgeman Art Library (cr). **94 Alamy Images:** Interfoto (tl); Lebrecht Music and Arts Photo Library (r). **Corbis:** Stapleton Collection (bc). **95 Corbis:** Stapleton Collection (br). **Dreamstime.com:** Rudchenko (cra). **Photo SCALA, Florence:** BPK, Bildagentur fuer Kunst, Kultur und Geschichte, Berlin (tr). **96 Alamy Images:** Robert Harding Picture Library Ltd (tr). **Allen Douglas, www.allendouglasstudio.com**. **The Art Archive:** Biblioteca Nazionale Marciana Venice / Gianni Dagli Orti (br, bl). **97 Alamy Images:** Mary Evans Picture Library (tl). **The Bridgeman Art Library:** Private Collection (br/griffin). **Corbis:** Alinari Archives (tr); Arte & Immagini srl (cr). **The Art Archive:** Biblioteca Nazionale Marciana Venice / Gianni Dagli Orti (bl, br). **O. Væring Picture Archive:** (cl). **98 Alamy Images:** World History Archive (c). **Corbis:** Historical Picture Archive (br, bc/agni, bl, bl/indra, bl/varuna). **Dreamstime.com:** Clairev (tl). **Getty Images:** elliott, elliott (tr); Photosindia (cl). **98-99 Fotolia:** sunshine (background). **99 Alamy Images:** Art Directors & TRIP (tr); Robert Harding Picture Library Ltd (bl); Louise Batalla Duran (tl); Tim Gainey (c). **Dorling Kindersley:** St Mungo, Glasgow Museums (br). **100 Alamy Images:** Art Directors & TRIP (cl/ saraswati); Angelo Hornak (bc); IndiaVisuals (bl); Bjorn Svensson (clb); Louise Batalla Duran (cl/kali). **101 Alamy Images:** Art Directors & TRIP. **Fotolia:** Sunshine (background). **102-103 Dreamstime.com:** Milos Tasic (background). **103 Tanya Goen, Made by Telaine:** (bl). **Visipix.com:** (tr). **104 Alamy Images:** The Art Gallery Collection (cla); Mary Evans Picture Library (b). **Dreamstime. com:** Splinex (tl). **Getty Images:** DEA / Veneranda Biblioteca Ambrosiana (c). **105 Dreamstime.com:** Rudchenko (br/ paper). **Yannis "Rubus" Roumboulias, http:// rubusthebarbarian.deviantart.com**. **The Art Archive:** Bibliothèque des Arts Décoratifs Paris / Gianni Dagli Orti (br). **106 Alamy Images:** The Art Gallery Collection (t). **Getty**

Images: The Bridgeman Art Library (bl). Jeroen Vogtschmidt: (br). 107 akg-images: (br). The Bridgeman Art Library: Private Collection / © Look and Learn (bl). Verónica Martínez Medellín: (tr). C. Henry Sanderson: (tl). 108 Alamy Images: Pick and Mix Images (tl). Tobias Kwan: (r). 110-111 Allen Douglas, www. allendouglasstudio.com: (b). Dreamstime.com: Milos Tasic (background). 110 Adam Vehige: (bl). 111 The Bridgeman Art Library: Palazzo Sandi-Porto (Cipollato), Venice, Italy (cr). Dreamstime.com: Rudchenko (cr/paper). 112 Alamy Images: Mary Evans Picture Library (c); Interfoto (tr); Mark Sykes (cl); North Wind Picture Archives (cr). Corbis: Historical Picture Archive (bl). Dreamstime.com: Clairev (tl). Getty Images: Gary Sludden (cla). Photo SCALA, Florence: BPK, Bildagentur fuer Kunst, Kultur und Geschichte, Berlin (br). The Art Archive: Palazzo Pitti Florence / Collection Dagli Orti (bc). 113 Alamy Images: Mary Evans Picture Library (tr, cb, bc); Peter Horree (tl); Interfoto (ca); Ivy Close Images (clb). The Bridgeman Art Library: Ashmolean Museum, University of Oxford, UK (crb); Private Collection (cra). Corbis: The Art Archive (bl); Ocean (br); The Gallery Collection (cla). Getty Images: DEA / G. Dagli Orti (family tree). 114 The Bridgeman Art Library: Private Collection / © Look and Learn (tl); Private Collection (cl). The Art Archive: Musée du Louvre Paris / Gianni Dagli Orti (tc). 114-115 Dreamstime.com: Mishoo (background). 115 akg-images: (br); Peter Connolly (cr). The Bridgeman Art Library: Private Collection / © Look and Learn (bl). Corbis: PoodlesRock (l). 116 akg-images: (c). The Bridgeman Art Library: Bolton Museum and Art Gallery, Lancashire, UK (l); Musee des Beaux-Arts, Marseille, France / Giraudon (br). Dreamstime.com: Splinex (tl). 117 akg-images. 118 Alamy Images: Interfoto (tr). The Bridgeman Art Library: Bibliotheque des Arts Decoratifs, Paris, France / Archives Charmet (l); Bibliotheque de L'Arsenal, Paris, France / Archives Charmet (br). 119 akg-images: (t). Alamy Images: Peter Horree (cr). Allen Douglas, www.allendouglasstudio.com: (br). TopFoto. co.uk: Ullstein Bild (bl). 120-121 Noel D Hill, www.ndhill. com. Courtesy of www.pieceofeight.com: (background). 120 Paul Carrington: (tc). The Art Archive: British Library (tl). 121 Alamy Images: Ivy Close Images (tr). www. stormthecastle.com: (br). 122 The Bridgeman Art Library: Birmingham Museums and Art Gallery (b); Private Collection / The Stapleton Collection (l). Getty Images: The Bridgeman Art Library (c). 123 The Bridgeman Art Library: Private Collection / The Stapleton Collection (cla, clb, bc, br, crb, t); Private Collection (bl). Corbis: Blue Lantern Studio (cra). Dreamstime.com: Rudchenko (tl/paper). Photolibrary: Britain on View (c). 124 akg-images: North Wind Picture Archives (tl). The Bridgeman Art Library: Derby Museum and Art Gallery, UK (b). Corbis: Stapleton Collection (tr). 125 Alamy Images: Interfoto (br). Stephanie M. Tan: (bl). The Art Archive: Victoria and Albert Museum London / Eileen Tweedy (t). 126-127 Alamy Images: Mary Evans Picture Library. 126 Dreamstime.com: Splinex. The Art Archive: Archaeological Museum Aleppo Syria / Gianni Dagli Orti (l). 127 Alamy Images: Ivy Close Images (tr). Corbis: Stapleton Collection (br). Dreamstime.com: Rudchenko (tl). 128 akg-images: Johann Brandstetter (b). Laura Csajagi: (t). 129 Alamy Images: Mary Evans Picture Library (tl, cr); Robert Harding Picture Library Ltd (cl). The Bridgeman Art Library: Ashmolean Museum, University of Oxford, UK (tr). Corbis: Bettmann (br). 130 Alamy Images: Porky Pies Photography (tc, br). The Bridgeman Art Library: Museo del Oro, Bogota, Colombia / © Paul Maeyaert (bl, tl). CGTextures.com: (l). Dreamstime.com: Rudchenko (bc/paper). 131 Gerard Miley. 132 The Bridgeman Art Library: (cl); Private Collection / © Look and Learn (b). Dreamstime.com: Splinex (tl). TopFoto.co. uk: Fortean (t); The British Library / HIP (cr). 133 The Bridgeman Art Library: Private Collection / © Look and Learn. Corbis: Blue Lantern Studio (b). 134-135 Getty Images: Alex Shahmiri Photography / Flickr (background). 135 akg-images: ullstein bild (br). Alamy Images: Danita Delimont (cl); Emmanuel Lattes (tl). The Bridgeman Art Library: Pinoteca Civica di Fano, Fano, Italy (tr). Corbis: Bob Rowan; Progressive Image (b). 136 Dreamstime.com: Milos Tasic. 137 Corbis: Bob Winsett. 138 The Bridgeman Art Library: Private Collection / The Stapleton Collection (c). Corbis: Gianni Dagli Orti (b). TopFoto.co.uk: The Granger Collection (t). 139 Alamy Images: Peter Horree (tl). The Bridgeman Art Library: Private Collection (b). Jisuk Cho: (tr). 140 Dreamstime.com: Lianquan Yu (bc). 140-141 CGTextures.com: (background). 141 Dreamstime.com: Dr.alex (t). 143 Verónica Martínez Medellín. 144 Dreamstime.com: Noel Powell (background). Island Art Publishers: Thunderbird and Killer Whale, by Joe Wilson (c).

All other images © Dorling Kindersley
For further information see: www.dkimages.com